I0102310

The Instant Voyeur

The Instant Voyeur

The Instant Voyeur

A Titillating Peek at Sex and Love

by

Tanya Slover

The Instant Voyeur:
A Titillating Peek at Sex and Love

First Edition 2012
Published by Invisibird Books

Interior images © www.arttoday.com
www.clipart.com

Cover Design by Tanya Slover

ISBN-13: 978-0615637341
ISBN-10: 0615637345

Invisibird
Books

Foreword

The Instant Voyeur: A Titillating Peek at Sex and Love offers up a lot of offbeat trivia about the worst and best in human behavior throughout our history. What you will read in this book is often provocative, sometimes outrageous, but never boring or lurid. It is merely an entertaining account of the two most enduring subjects on earth - sex and love.

Though I have researched and verified the information in these pages to the best of my ability, *The Instant Voyeur* is obviously tongue in cheek and meant to be entertaining, not scholarly - an enjoyable way to pick up interesting tidbits to share at parties, the office and with your Facebook friends.

I hope you enjoy the read.

The Instant Voyeur

What clever device did streetwalkers employ in ancient Greece to solicit business?

They wore sandals with the words, *Follow Me*, studded on their soles.

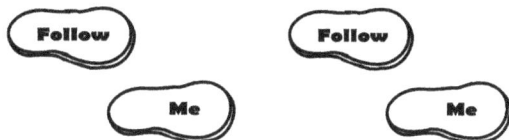

Why is the wedding ring worn on the third finger?

The so-called "ring finger" was believed to be the origin of a vein - the *vena amoris*, or "vein of love" - that traveled from the third finger to the heart. The custom, which began in early Rome, signified a couple had joined hearts and lives forever.

What hormone may be responsible for inducing feelings of love?

Oxytocin. Triggered by either physical or emotional stimuli (a glance, a smile, etc.), this love hormone makes people want to fondle and cuddle each other. As arousal builds, so does the level of *oxytocin* in one's body, maxing out at the moment of orgasm.

Who philosophized, "At the touch of love everyone becomes a poet"?

Plato.

What supposed romantic gesture inspired the invention of the champagne glass?

After a regrettable spat with his mistress, King Louis XIV of France (r. 1643-1715) was said to have had a mold cast of one of her breasts and a glass fashioned from it.* The shape of that glass purportedly resembles some of the ones we sip champagne from today.

* Louis XIV had many mistresses - so exactly which one was the inspiration is anyone's guess.

What creatures participate in a "penis fencing" match before they mate?

Hermaphroditic flatworms. At least one species rears up when encountering his/her beloved, sticks out its penis and tries to jab the other one with it. The flatworm that is poked first loses the "penile duel" and gets fertilized by the winner's sperm. The loser is then stuck with having the baby worms.

Why were a virgin's bones used in the construction of medieval buildings?

When mixed with mortar, the bones of virgins were believed to protect castles, churches and fortresses from all enemies and all harm. If the structure failed, it meant the girl lied.

What made the 1970 best-selling book, *The Sensuous Woman*, so popular?

It featured a whole chapter on fellatio. Authored by a woman called "J," the book's famous Eleventh Chapter detailed such techniques as "The Butterfly Flick," "The Chinese Tickle" and "The Whipped Cream Wriggle."

What powerful New York state politician was busted for "sexting" in 2011 and ultimately resigned from the U.S. House of Representatives?

The U.S. Democratic Congressman, Anthony Weiner. Randy Andy used Twitter to send explicit pictures of his private endowment to various women. When he was outed for tweeting the pictures, Weiner initially denied it saying his Twitter account had been hacked. He alternatively claimed that the photos in question were doctored. Amid the media storm that followed and the graphic postings of his penis going viral on the internet, Weiner finally admitted he did the tweets and stepped down. As of 2012, Weiner let be known he wanted back into politics.

After a long, passionate affair, what famous medieval lovers took religious vows and then remained celibate for the rest of their lives?

Abelard and Heloise. After the renowned scholar, Abelard, was castrated by friends of Heloise's uncle for dishonoring his niece, he became a monk and she, a nun. Their passion then took the form of letters to each other. Heloise once said she would have followed Abelard "to hell itself" since he was not only master of her body, but of her soul as well. These twelfth-century lovers are now buried together in the Pere Lachaise Cemetery in Paris.

What saintly soul made the observation, "If you judge people, you have no time to love them"?

Mother Teresa.

What candy contains a chemical much like one our own bodies produce when we're in love?

Chocolate. Hershey's Kisses got it right a long time ago. *Phenylethylamine*, a chemical produced in the brain, apparently increases when people fall in love.

Who reportedly said "I love Mickey Mouse more than any woman I've ever known," and probably meant it?

Walt Disney. Apparently, Minnie didn't count.

What erotic love manual, one of the most graphic ever written on the subject of sex, classifies a man's lingum (penis) according to its size?

The *Kama Sutra,* also known as *The Hindu Art of Love*, written by Vatsyayana around the second century A.D. and translated into English in 1883 by Sir Richard Francis Burton. The size classifications for a man's *lingum* are: hare, bull or horse man. A woman's *yoni* is divided into three sizes according to its depth: female deer, mare or elephant.

Note: The book also contains many pretzel-twisting positions for making love and features a detailed section on aphrodisiacs.

What does the zealous "Dirty Girls Ministries" crusade against?

The evils of female masturbation. Launched in 2009, the online ministry purportedly helps women recover from

11

their addictions to that unholy trinity: romance novels, masturbation and pornography.

What infamous 18ᵗʰ-century pornographer was dug up after his death so his head could be examined?

The Marquis de Sade. Some 20 years after his death in 1814, the man who perfected sexual cruelty and whose very name is responsible for the introduction of the word sadism into our vocabulary was exhumed so his skull could be examined. Phrenology, or the study of the shape and bumps on a person's head to determine their character, was in vogue at the time. Some of those who analyzed the Marquis's head decided it probably belonged to a priest.

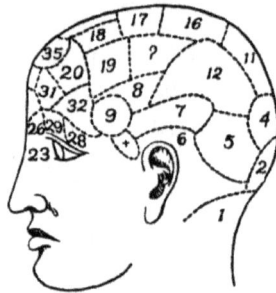

Note: Sade's sexual proclivities (flagellation, sodomy and group sex to mention three) and powerful enemies (not the least of whom was his mother-in-law) landed him in jail for 27 of his 74 years. It was during his repeated incarcerations that the "Divine Marquis" penned most of his graphic tales of sexuality, perversion and torture, including *Justine* and *120 Days of Sodom*.

What best-selling book is brimming with accounts of homosexuality, incest, rape, sadism, prostitution and adultery?

The Bible.

How do fireflies get each other's amorous attention?

They use a "blinking code." The specific blinking pattern one species employs is designed to attract a mate. However, some species have evolved into predators and have learned to mimic the patterns of other fireflies so they can eat them. Not knowing whether one is going to be loved or eaten from one moment to the next must undoubtedly provide for some very anxious firefly moments.

Note: A substance called *luciferin* is responsible for all the firefly pyrotechnics. Present in luminescent organisms, *luciferin* produces light when it is combined with oxygen in the presence of an oxidizing enzyme called *luciferase*.

What is parthenophobia?

Fear of virgins.

What comedian reportedly once said of male sexuality, "See, the problem is that God gives men a brain and a penis, and only enough blood to run one at a time"?

Robin Williams

What deceased person's heart did *Frankenstein* author, Mary Shelley, keep on her desk?

Her beloved husband's - the famous romantic poet, Percy Bysshe Shelley.

What were Victorian brides told on their wedding day?

"Lie still and think of the Empire."

Which English Queen was said to have inadvertently approved of lesbianism in the 1800s?

Queen Victoria. It has been widely and erroneously circulated that when a bill was brought to her that would make homosexuality illegal, she had all female references to such behavior deleted refusing to accept that it even existed. In so doing she outlawed male homosexuality and indirectly sanctioned lesbianism. Amusing, but not true.

What well-known, macho actor's film debut was in a porn flick?

Sylvester Stallone. He played the lead in *Party at Kitty and Studs* released in 1970 and was paid $200 for it.

What is poetically referred to as "The Sweet Death"?

Orgasm, *la mort douce*, as the French have called it.

In what marine species does the male have the babies?

The seahorse. The female deposits her eggs into his pouch where they are fertilized by his sperm. His body then gestates them to term.

Where was prostitution once considered sacred?

In ancient Greece and Rome. Sex was a holy rite then. A state of grace was conferred on the man who paid to have this piety performed on him. The money earned was used to maintain the temple and provide for the sacred prostitutes who lived there.

Relative to its body size what land creature has one of the largest penises on earth?

The flea. Relative penile proportions to body size vary greatly in the literature. Some say twice, others more.

Are the chemical changes love produces in the brain visible to certain imaging devices?

Yes. In one experiment when volunteers were shown pictures of their true love and then had an MRI taken of their brains, identifiable chemical changes occurred that did not take place when those same volunteers were shown pictures of their friends. Apparently, these are the same areas of the brain that respond to cocaine and other "euphoric states."

What is one of the purported derivations of the word, "hooker"?

The word's usage is often linked with Joseph Hooker, a Union general during the Civil War. To keep his men's spirits up during hostilities, General Hooker reportedly allowed prostitutes into camp and let them "fraternize" with his troops. "Hooker's girls," as some called them, continued working after the Civil War and Hooker's name has followed them ever since.

What former Prime Minister of England observed, "The magic of our first love is our ignorance that it can ever end"?

Benjamin Disraeli.

What aquatic Romeo is able to croon love songs to his sweetheart across a hundred miles of ocean?

The humpback whale.

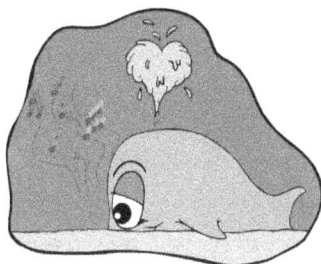

"Wet dreams" aside, is an orgasm possible without any genital contact?

Yes. Spontaneous orgasms, as they are called, occur with no physical contact. People report spontaneously achieving a climax while watching movies, exercising, reading and having certain fantasies and/or erotic thoughts - all without the benefit of genital or hands-on stimulation.

Who was the "Mayflower Madam"?

Sydney Biddle Barrows, the head of an exclusive New York City escort service from 1979 to 1984 called *Cachet*. It catered to the rich and powerful - diplomats, oil sheiks, high-rollers from business and finance, etc. Barrows said what made her business so successful was that she hired the very best and paid them what they were worth.

Note: The press used the catchy sobriquet, Mayflower Madam, because Barrows' ancestors had come over on the Mayflower.

In what Western country was killing one's spouse for adultery still an acceptable defense until the twentieth century?

France. A *crime passionel*, or crime of passion, was a sure-fire bet for acquittal if someone caught their husband or wife fooling around. This defense, however, seemed to work better for men.

What famous bad boy actor, aficionado of prostitution, reportedly said, "You're not paying a hooker to have sex. You're paying her to leave afterwards"?

Charlie Sheen, the ex-star of *Two and a Half Men.*

What did playwright Charles MacArthur supposedly say to the first lady of the American stage, Helen Hays, upon first meeting her at a party?

While offering her some peanuts he uttered the inspired line, "I only wish they were emeralds." Another version of that romantic encounter was, "If only they were emeralds." Whatever MacArthur's exact words, they were apparently irresistible. They led right to the altar.

What is a merkin?

It's a pubic wig. Women supposedly started wearing merkins in the mid-1600s, maybe even earlier. Why? No one seems quite sure. Some think it was possibly because a heavy lice infestation at the time made it desirable to sport a bald-pated pube. Merkins, it seems, were reserved for special occasions, whatever those were.

What very infamous Renaissance Pope, along with his equally infamous children, hosted a rollicking party at the papal palace on October 1, 1501, and is said to have told the 50 prostitutes they had invited to take off their clothes, get down on their hands and feet and retrieve, as best they could, the chestnuts which had been tossed among randomly placed, lighted candles?

The imaginative party animals were Pope Alexander VI and his fun-loving kids, Lucretia and Cesare Borgia. A contest was announced that same night that was won by the man who had sex the greatest number of times. According to Havelock Ellis's book, *Sex in Relation to Society*, this party is just one more example of Alexander's debauched papal court. Burchard, the pope's own secretary, recorded the details of the evening in his diary and is Ellis's source for the account.

Where is the world's largest collection of pornographic literature rumored to reside?

None other than the Vatican Library. This rumor has persisted for centuries. The Vatican denies such a trove exists or ever existed. Most serious researchers also agree that the Vatican was probably never into serious smut.

When did the first "lesbian" novel appear in print?

In the 18ᵗʰ century, 1788 to be exact. *Mary, A Fiction*, was written by Mary Wollstonecraft, the mother of Mary Shelley, author of *Frankenstein*. The novel tells of one woman's passionate and fierce attachment to a female friend. Though devoid of direct allusions to a physical relationship, the women did sleep together in the same bed. Other than this novel, Wollstonecraft produced three pieces of very important nonfiction: *A Vindication of the Rights of Women; A Vindication of the Rights of Men*; and, *Historical and Moral View of the Origin and Progress of the French Revolution.*

Note: A short story, or novella, about a group of lesbian nuns appeared in France in 1682. Called *Venus in the Cloister*, a few prurient purists might consider this the first lesbian tale in literature.

What dangerous and respected job did Norma Jean Almodovar have before she quit it in 1984 to become a prostitute?

She was a Los Angeles police officer. After she quit the LAPD and became a prostitute she said she had done so because it "was far more honest work than working for the police department." She apparently witnessed rampant corruption in the LAPD and was very vocal about it. *Cop to Call Girl,* published in 1993 by Simon & Schuster, is a detailed, no-holds-barred account of Almodovar's career choices.

How did the men of the Walibri tribe of Central Australia once greet each other?

By shaking penises, whether their own or each other's couldn't be verified.

What did Noah Webster, the founding father of *The American Dictionary*, change the word "testicles" to?

Peculiar members. A Victorian prude and religious nut, Mr. Webster replaced a lot of "indelicate" words in his dictionary with euphemisms. He also took it upon himself to clean up The Holy Bible's "offending" language and produced a sanitized version in 1833. The sacred tome's "go a-whoring" was rendered "go astray;" "buttocks" became "hind parts," and the term, "private parts," was renamed "peculiar members," designating testicles, in particular, among its peculiars.

What is a "Spanish Fly"?

Once mistakenly touted as an aphrodisiac, the term refers to a substance extracted from the *Cantharides* or Spanish "blister beetle" called *cantharidin.* The so-called love potion made from this is potentially very dangerous capable of causing severe urogenital irritation, including permanent kidney damage and even death.

Why did some Nevada brothels reportedly experience a sharp, upward turn in their 1998 business?

Viagra. More customers simply became available.

Who was one of the best-paid hookers of all time?

Renaissance courtesan, polemicist and poet, Veronica Franco. Just one night with her reportedly cost a small fortune as she was coveted not only for her extraordinary sexual talents but for her mental gifts as well. The film *Dangerous Beauty* recounts part of Veronica's fascinating life as a prostitute and as an influential "citizen poet" in sixteenth-century Venice.

What gets removed when a man is castrated?

In some instances only the testicles are cut off while in others, there is complete removal of all genitalia. Such was the case in China at one time. The testicles and the penis were "shaved off," leaving nothing but an orifice through which to urinate. In the Middle East it was also common to remove all the genitalia since men who had only been testicularly castrated (especially after puberty) could not be trusted to guard the sultan's harem.* They might still be able to get an erection and have long-lasting, orgasmless sex. In fact, the castrati or castrated opera singers of the seventeenth and eighteenth centuries were frequently sought out as lovers. Not only could they hit high C, they could hold it. Additionally, their women lovers had no fear of pregnancy.

* Eunuch is derived from the Greek, "guardian or keeper of the bed."

Who has observed to the disquiet of many that "We exaggerate the sexual appetite in ourselves to take the place of the love we inadequately feel"?

Writer Graham Greene.

What notorious Roman emperor openly flaunted his passion for a man and even married him?

Nero. He tied the knot with his eunuch, Sporus, in a public ceremony in Rome. Nero claimed Sporus, who loved dressing up as a woman and parading down the street, resembled his deceased wife. Not all Romans agreed with the Emperor's spin on his new marriage and were put off by his public demonstrations of affection toward his new spouse.

What arachnid practices sexual cannibalism?

The black widow. But there are other arachnids and insects that practice it as well. After mating, the black widow gratefully gobbles up her mate.

Why did women in ancient Egypt sometimes urinate on grain seed?

To see if they were pregnant. Two different types of grain seed were used. If either one sprouted, the test was positive. The sex of the child was foretold by which of the two seeds it was. The test was purportedly 70% accurate.

Who so aptly wrote of the misbehaving penis, "...it does what it desires; and often the man is asleep and it is awake, and many times the man is awake and it is asleep; many times the man wishes it to practice and it does not wish it; many times it wishes it and the man forbids it"?

Leonardo da Vinci (circa 1500 A.D.).

What were some synonyms for prick in 18th-century England?

In Francis Grose's 1785 book, *A Classical Dictionary of the Vulgar Tongue*, a prick by any other name was a lobcock, plug tail, stargazer, sugar stick or whorepipe.

Where was a concoction of honey and crocodile dung once used as a female contraceptive?

Ancient Egypt. The unlikely blend was inserted in the vagina before sex and not only blocked any sperm from fertilizing an egg but probably killed them as well due to the dung's high acid content. The potent potion appears to be one of the world's first successful spermicides.

Note: Cleopatra supposedly inserted stones in her vagina to prevent conception.

Why did some medieval chastity belts sport an array of spring-loaded "teeth?"

To make sure not a single finger dare poke or prod where it ought not. In the Middle Ages missing digits could be interpreted as proof of misbehaving. Needless to say, the ladies didn't fool around while those who held the key to their virtue were away on crusade - not even with themselves.

Men in what South African tribe have a semi-erect, or horizontal, penis at all times?

The Bushmen of the Kalahari Desert in Botswana. Why this characteristic evolved among the Bushmen in the first place is a source of endless speculation. Some anthropologists think the "semi-erection" may have initially been a genetic response to the very well endowed *mons pubis* (fleshy mound at lower part of the abdomen) of the tribe's women. In any event, neighboring tribes in the Kalahari have found the attribute a source of much amusement, much to the annoyance of the Bushmen.

What great twentieth-century statesman was rumored to have gotten down on all fours when he was in the mood, crawled over to his wife's door and caterwauled like a tomcat?

Winston Churchill. Apocryphal or not, this story makes for a very amusing visual.

What overly amorous insect gnaws her partner's head off during mating?

The praying mantis. In some species the male mantis continues mating even after being decapitated, sometimes for hours.

How many women did Errol Flynn reportedly claim to have had sex with?

13,000. Puffery, who knows? Maybe his accounting didn't include just one score a night and, believe it or not, followers of that titillating who's-been-with-whom list say the figure is low.

Note: Mick Jagger has purportedly bedded 4,000+ women and Wilt Chamberlain, the NBA star, circa 20,000. Obviously, these guys cannot help but sleep and tell.

What is the "G-spot" and where is it located?

The Grafenberg*, or G-spot, is a highly sensitive area inside the vagina whose stimulation reportedly produces a deeper, more intense orgasm than clitoral ones and causes a urethral ejaculation in some women. In case you're interested, the magic spot is located near the urethra on the front vaginal wall.

* Ernest Grafenberg was the German physician who invented the Grafenberg ring, a precursor of today's IUDs. While researching his "ring," he happened upon the "the spot."

What world-class pharmacy, said to be one of the most pharmacologically complete, does not carry Viagra?

The Vatican City Pharmacy in Vatican City. No need to wonder why.

What celebrated wit once remarked, "I've tried several varieties of sex. The conventional position makes me claustrophobic. And the others either give me a stiff neck or lockjaw"?

Tallulah Bankhead.

Who were considered the most learned, cultured and sexually liberated women of the ancient world?

The *hetairai* or Greek courtesans. These women were sought out not only for sex but also for their wit and intellect. Quite unlike the wives of the husbands they entertained, the *hetairai* were allowed to sit at the table with men and take part in their conversations.

In what famous classical play did women go on a "sex strike" so men would stop warring with each other?

Lysistrata, a comedy written circa 411 B.C. by Greek playwright Aristophanes. The strike worked. Perhaps its sentiments inspired the 1960s' hippie cry, "Make love, not war."

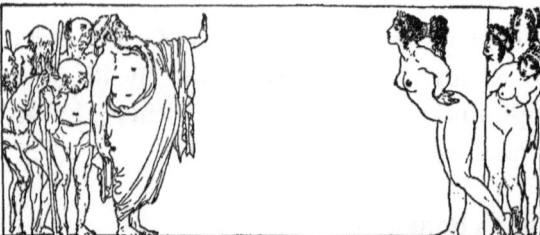

Why was the French artist Henri de Toulouse-Lautrec given the nickname of "Teapot"?

Other than his legs which were grievously stunted by childhood injuries, the rest of Toulouse-Lautrec's body was of normal proportions. As a result, the women at the Moulin Rouge conferred the moniker on him. Others say he was so named because he was a very short fellow with a very large spout; i.e., a well-endowed penis.

Who believed the dead could impregnate the living?

The ancient Egyptians. It was believed that a mummy could father a child after death just as the god, Osiris, had fathered Horus.

What is usually considered the most dangerous time for someone at risk of a heart attack to have sex?

Upon first awakening.

What famous 18th-century French poet defined love as "an oasis of horror in a desert of boredom"?

Charles Baudelaire – ever the charming cynic.

What notorious eighteenth-century lover wrote many scholarly books, translated the *Iliad* into French (among other great classics) and had countless careers, including that of a dancer, spy, priest, cook, violinist, cat burglar and librarian?

Casanova.   In view of all his occupations it's a wonder he had time to make love to anyone. He was born Giacomo Girolamo Casanova in Venice, Italy, in 1725, and died 1798 in Czechoslovakia. Penniless in his later years, Casanova ended up working as a librarian in Castle Dux (now called Duchcov) in a very isolated region of Northern Bohemia north of Prague. It was during this time Casanova penned his 3,700 page memoir, *Story of My Life,* about his innumerable sexual escapades and entanglements all over Europe and Russia.*   In the preface he writes, "I was born for the opposite sex. I have always loved it and done all that I could to make myself loved by it." At one time promoted for its voyeuristic titillation, Casanova's autobiography is now being considered for its literary merit by scholars all over the world.

 * Casanova got around, not just with the ladies but geographically as well. It is estimated he traveled some 40,000 miles during his lifetime over rutted, often almost impassable, roads by stagecoach.

In Greece who was a young virgin required to have sex with before sleeping with her husband?

With Priapus, the Greek god personifying the male procreative power. Once "deflowered" by her lover god, a woman could then sleep with her husband.

What condition produces an unrelenting hard-on?

Priapism, so named for the Greek god, Priapus. This abnormality often occurs without sexual excitement and results in a very painful and persistent erection of the penis. If not resolved, the penile tissue may die.

What is erotomania?

The delusion that one is loved or desired by someone else when, in fact, such feelings may never have been even remotely entertained by the love object. The erotomaniac interprets everything the supposed lover says or does - any action, look, gesture, word - as a confirmation of his/her affection and interest toward them. The condition can be serious and may require psychiatric intervention. Many stalkers are erotomaniacs, convinced that those they desire somehow also desire them - although they may have never met.

What famous poet obsessed for over 30 years about a lady he glimpsed in church one day but never actually met?

Petrarch. On April 6, l327, the poet was instantly smitten when he saw "Laura" in the Church of Santa

Chiara in Avignon, France. Petrarch's "unmet beloved" soon became the inspiration for some of the most famous sonnets* in literature. When the Black Death (bubonic plague) claimed Laura in 1348, a deeply grieving Petrarch continued to immortalize her in writing until his own death in 1374.

* Simply called *The Sonnets*, Petrarch wrote hundreds of them to his unmet beloved.

Which President had repeated sexual encounters in a very tiny White House closet?

Warren G. Harding (1921-1923). In her book, *The President's Daughter**, Nan Britton describes her many cramped assignations with Mr. Harding.

* The tell-all book by Nan Britton claims that her daughter, Elizabeth Ann, was fathered by President Harding.

"Choking the chicken" refers to what often-practiced autoerotic activity?

Male masturbation.

Who said the following to her dying lover?

Kiss me yet once again, the last, long kiss,
Until I draw your soul within my lips
And drink down all your love.

Aphrodite, the Goddess of Love and Beauty. They were the last words she spoke to handsome, young Adonis after he was fatally gored by a wild boar. The red anemone, which was said to have sprung up where Adonis shed his blood, became the beloved flower of Greek girls, celebrated by them everywhere it bloomed.

What is a sex addict?

Someone whose drug of choice is sex. Just like people with other addictions, satisfaction of a sex addict's compulsion can only be achieved by getting a "fix," or more sex.

What early Church theologian and saint advocated procreation "without the excitement of lust"?

St. Augustine. Lustful beyond measure himself as a young man, St. Augustine suddenly swore off sex at 33 and converted to Christianity. Ordained a priest in 391 A.D., he continued to expound his curious ideas about human sexuality. To his new way of thinking, sex was acceptable only for procreation and must not be enjoyed or it was a sin. St. Augustine's views influenced Western culture for centuries and still do.

If a man is diagnosed with *satyriasis*, what's he got?

He has an abnormal, uncontrollable urge for sexual intercourse.

What is a draggletail?

A whore of yore.

What device worn in Europe during the fifteenth and sixteenth centuries exaggerated the size of man's penis?

The codpiece. Worn outside the pants, this medieval designer item not only bulged suggestively but was sometimes decorated with a snake or a gargoyle's head to draw even more attention to the manly wares beneath.

When did wedding cakes first make their appearance?

Rome, probably sometime in the first century A.D. The cakes* were originally not eaten but thrown. Wheat, long a symbol of fecundity, was baked into the cakes and used to pelt the bride. Eventually, the guests realized it was more enjoyable to eat the cakes and started throwing rice instead to bless the bride's untested fertility.

* Unlike the present day multi-tiered ones, these first-century wedding cakes were quite small.

What legendary medieval temple has explicit erotic art sculpted on its walls?

The Sun Temple of Konark (also known as the Black Pagoda) located south of Calcutta. This Hindu temple is covered with erotic carvings depicting almost every sexual position you can think of and some you probably haven't. Many believe this stone erotica was inspired by *The Kama Sutra*.

What is meant by "The Right of the First Night"?

A custom that dates back thousands of years, it gave the lord of the manor the right to spend the first night with any newly married woman in his domain. Some lords even charged the bridegroom a fee for "deflowering" his new bride. The first historical mention of the "lord's right" appears in the *The Epic of Gilgamesh*, an epic poem about a Mesopotamian king called Gilgamesh who slept with every new bride in his kingdom.

Note: Under the ancient Romans the custom was called *jus primae noctis* and later, during feudal times, *droit de seigneur*. In the antebellum South it was known as "the master's obligation." Under this "obligation," the white plantation owner asserted his "right" to sleep with his black female slaves on their wedding night and other times as well. Some scholars say such a *droit* never existed. As is always the case, the experts disagree.

What is "the love that dare not speak its name"?

Homosexuality. "I am the love that dare not speak its name," was contained in a poem entitled *Two Loves* written by Alfred Lord Douglas. Lord Douglas or "Bosie," as Oscar Wilde liked to call him, was the young man initially responsible for Wilde's legal woes in 1895. The scandal and outrage over their affair led to a trial and Wilde's imprisonment for two years.

What 19ᵗʰ-century "vice" supposedly led to impotence, baldness and muscular atrophy?

Masturbation. Men were told that such sexual self-abuse would poison their nervous system and could end in dementia and/or suicide. Remedies for "the secret vice" included special diets, infibulation (a special operation involving the foreskin), electric shock and endless elixirs.

Note: The Male Chastity Belt, patented by Michael McCormick in 1898, claimed it could prevent self-abuse. The apparatus worked by means of multiple "pricking-points" (no pun intended) located along an adjustable sliding plate strapped to the penis.

What lucrative business did members of the clergy own during the Middle Ages?

"Public houses" - now known as whorehouses. One bishop reportedly had so many prostitutes working for him he lost count.

Mary Wollstonecraft, author of the radical 18ᵗʰ-century feminist work, *A Vindication of the Rights of Women* (first published in 1792), was the mother of what very famous daughter?

Mary Shelley, author of *Frankenstein*. Mother and daughter both believed in women's rights and "free love."

What is the Biblical sin of onanism?

Coitus interruptus or withdrawal before ejaculation.

In the book of Genesis, Judah's son, Onan, withdraws from his brother's wife (a widow) and spills his "seed" on the ground. The action so displeased the Lord that He "slew" Onan and sperm wasting was made a sin.

What religious leader conned his female parishioners into having sex with him during the 1930s and 40s with the self-serving counsel, "I am bringing your desire to the surface so that I can eliminate it"?

Father Divine aka George Baker aka God, who ultimately proved himself more expert at seduction than sermonizing.

What aristocratic, rich and eccentric French writer once admitted he needed to watch starved rats viciously tear and claw at each other before he could achieve orgasm?

Marcel Proust (1871-1922), author of the reflective and monumentally long novel, *Remembrance of Things Past*. It is said he told Andre Gide, a fellow writer and friend, that he often used such horrors to intensify his sensations while masturbating or he couldn't climax. No wonder Mr. Proust never quite succeeded at romance.

What 19th-century group practiced free love in Upstate New York?

The Oneida Community. Founded in 1848 by John Humphrey Noyes, the commune was joined together in a "complex marriage" which theoretically gave everyone the right to have sex with everyone else in the group. The

Oneidans believed the utopia they were seeking could be found through the practice of free love. The men in the community were taught *coitus reservatus*, which, unlike *coitus interruptus*, meant the man did not ejaculate. Such sexual control supposedly allowed a couple to avoid propagation while exploring the deeper aspects of love. Oneidans also practiced *karezza*, derived from ancient Tantric and Taoist techniques, in which neither partner allowed himself or herself to climax. Such orgasmless sex was claimed to be the key to a deeper, more intimate union.

What mythical man followed his lover to hell and back?

Orpheus. Grief-stricken at Eurydice's death, he gains access to the underworld and persuades Hades to let his beloved return to the world of light. Impressed by the beautiful music Orpheus plays on his lute and the sincerity of his request, the master of hell agrees but stipulates one condition: Orpheus must not look back at Eurydice, not once, no matter what, as she follows him out of hell. Just as Orpheus steps once again into the light of the world, he eagerly glances back at his beloved Eurydice who, still following behind in the darkness, is then lost to him forever.

What Founding Father was quite the lady's man who respected the female intellect and, for the most part, championed women's rights?

Benjamin Franklin. Women were apparently crazy about him and actively sought out his company, including his sexual favors, way into his seventies. A ribald little essay he wrote on choosing a mistress so embarrassed Congress it spent taxpayer's dollars trying to buy up all the copies.

Note: Ben Franklin liked women every bit as much as Casanova. However, when the two Lotharios actually met in Paris, they supposedly discussed hot air balloons.

Has a castrated man ever had his penis successfully reattached?

Yes. Perhaps the most famous case is that of John Wayne Bobbitt. In 1993 his wife angrily bobbed his penis, then made a quick getaway with it and tossed the former love object of her affection out a car window. Luckily for him someone recovered the discarded member while it could still be surgically reattached. The operation was apparently a complete success. A year later, Mr. Bobbitt starred in an X-rated flick that demanded his very best and he gave it.

What is the origin of Valentine's Day?

Many myths and stories surround its genesis. One of the most touching is of an early Christian named Valentinus who was jailed for refusing to take part in pagan worship. While imprisoned, legend goes, he healed the jailer's daughter of blindness. Just prior to his execution on February 14th, Valentinus supposedly sent her a note signed, "Your Valentine." St. Valentine is now the patron saint of lovers.

Why did dancing almost disappear in Europe during the Middle Ages?

Believed to be an invention of the devil, the Church was sure the evil activity stimulated its flock's fornication impulses and discouraged dancing in every way possible.

Why did Romans consider seafood an aphrodisiac?

They reasoned that since Venus, the goddess of love, was born of the sea, food from its depths must surely put its partakers in an amorous mood.

Medieval German "love cakes" were prepared with what two main ingredients?

Semen and/or menstrual blood. The old Teutons believed that bodily secretions, when added to baked goods, had the power to induce love.

What religious sect does not allow its members to shake hands much less have sex?

The Shakers. Needless to say, there are not many adherents left. In 2011 there was reportedly just one.

Why do women go to doctors for "gummy bears"?

The so-called "gummy bear" implants approved in 2012 are being hailed by plastic surgeons as new "the holy grail" of artificial breasts. Apparently, they feel more natural than other implants and are less likely to break or harden. Ergo their name because, just like gummy bears, they supposedly remain supple and keep their shape.

What iconic actor said, "Love is the delightful interval between meeting a girl and discovering that she looks like a haddock"?

John Barrymore, Drew Barrymore's grandfather.

How did kissing begin?

By sniffing strangers, or so goes one theory. It was thought to be a way to size someone up. By smelling and/or tasting someone else, many ancient cultures believed you could gauge another person's mood, receptivity, etc. Sniffing ultimately evolved into kissing and a whole new way of sizing someone up began.

What French King was initially unable to consummate his marriage because of an abnormality of his foreskin?

King Louis XVI. *Phimosis*, or tightness of the foreskin, was the alleged cause of the King's sexual dysfunction. The condition results in an extremely painful erection which, when achieved at all, makes intercourse well nigh impossible. Louis's seven-year marriage to Marie Antoinette was reportedly consummated after he agreed to a simple operation to fix the problem.

What mythical creature can only be seen by a virgin?

A unicorn. There are many complex variants of the myth but in most the connection between the unicorn and chastity are present in some form or the other.

What do the following foods have in common: ginseng, celery, asparagus, truffles and, of course, oysters and caviar?

They are all considered aphrodisiacs to mention just a few in an extensive list.

What short showed the first kiss on film?

The Kiss. Made by Thomas Edison for nickelodeon audiences, the 1896 film ran about 30 seconds.

What Greek poet has been called "The Tenth Muse"?

Sappho. Male contemporaries conferred the epithet on her. Very sensual and controversial, Sappho's poetry was described by other less enthusiastic followers as lewd and licentious. Ovid attacked her work as nothing less than an instruction course in female homosexuality. Reay

Tannahill's book, *Sex in History*, gives the following sampling of Sappho's work:

Return, I implore thee, clad in thy milk-white tunic.
Ah, what intense desire attends thy beauteous form.
No woman could not but tremble at its seduction.

What debauched Roman Emperor supposedly kept his wife in line with the following threat as he kissed her neck, "Off comes this head whenever I give the word"?

Caligula (12-41 A.D.). It goes without saying - this guy wasn't noted for his benevolence or finesse with women. His sexual perversity and cruelty are legendary.

What 20ᵗʰ-century decade brought about a sea change in social attitudes regarding sexual behavior?

The 60s - the decade that launched the so-called sexual revolution. The Pill, along with the feminist and many other counterculture movements, student protests, etc., all said enough to America's repressive social mores. A revolution of mostly the young, sexual liberation became their battle cry for freedom. It was during this decade that the gay and lesbian movement took off in earnest, when so-called "sexual politics" defined a new direction for everyone and when the "love-in" became the protest of choice for voicing peaceful opposition. The 1968 rock musical, *Hair*, clearly confirmed the new sense of sexual freedom people were experiencing across the country when, at one point in the performance, the actors appeared naked on stage. However short it was on plot, *Hair* managed to capture the zeitgeist of the 1960s by touching on almost every social, political and sexual issue of the day.

What did monks in the Early Middle Ages do to prevent sexual arousal?

Among other things, they practiced regular bloodletting. They believed the retention of semen led to blood poisoning. If, after a particularly sanguineous session, a monk's blood revealed no impurities or gross matter, it meant he was having sex. Reprimands and penance quickly followed. So did more bloodletting.

What were cosmetics once called?

"Poultices of lust." An early Church cleric and fanatic named Jerome admonished all Christian women not to accentuate any attractiveness they might possess. Leading men astray was a big sin.

What country is usually credited with making the first movie showing unsimulated, on-screen sex?

Sweden. The film, *They Call Us Misfits*, is said to have premiered the real thing in 1967. Six years later the buzz had it that what the audience saw on screen between Julie Christie and Donald Sutherland in *Don't Look Now* was also the real thing. Sutherland has repudiated these stories claiming they were all just rumors, nothing more.

What was once meant by a glamor (formerly spelled glamour)?

A spell. If a witch cast a glamour upon a man, she might make his private parts disappear. Due to the hysteria at the time of The Inquisition, it was sometimes difficult convincing a man it was only an illusion - that his penis was still very much intact.

What did Jacqueline Kennedy Onassis have to say about sex?

Ever the fashion plate, she once remarked that "Sex is a bad thing because it rumples the clothes." Why she might have sex in them in the first place was never spelled out.

Who said, "If music be the food of love, play on"?

William Shakespeare

Who was George Jorgensen and what turned him into an overnight sensation in 1952?

He was the first ex-GI to become a real lady. In 1952 George went to Denmark and then returned as Christine Jorgensen, becoming a veteran of one of the first sex-change operations to be performed on an American man.

In what culture was a woman's orgasm considered just as important as a man's?

In that of the ancient and very wise Chinese.

Historically, what has the Catholic Church considered as an "unnatural lechery" between married people?

Fellatio and anal sex. At least that's what it decided back in the seventeenth century.

What blond bombshell provocateur claimed, "I do all my best work in bed"?

Mae West.

What sexual activity can help relieve depression?

Masturbation.

Where was widow burning once an accepted sacrificial practice?

India. In past centuries *sati**, or widow burning, was common after the death of privileged men in certain castes. Frequently, the wives and mistresses were cremated along with the deceased in a giant funeral pyre. One account from the 1800s describes how several wives and dancing girls were burned to death without a whimper. Another account said one Rajah was burned with over 60 of his wives. Apparently, the number of wives, concubines and assorted women willing to die in a princely bonfire spoke to his success in life.

* *Sati* was supposedly voluntary, emphasizing the faithfulness and devotion of a woman to her husband or keeper even in his death. Some eyewitness accounts, however, claim the women were most likely drugged with opium, not love and loyalty.

What things are you attracted to if you suffer from the condition known as *hierophilia*?

An attraction to sacred objects such as crosses, holy icons, etc. The disorder has a strong sexual component.

What condom was named after an Egyptian pharaoh?

Ramses.   It is estimated that Ramses II fathered between 100 and 180 kids suggesting he should have used the product his name bears.

In deference to delicacy, how did many Victorians refer to a chicken's breast?

As its "bosom."   Just imagine saying to someone, "Would you please pass me that chicken bosom?"

Why have women historically believed to be easy prey for the devil?

Carnal lust. The Church has long considered women to be sexually insatiable. It was thus assumed they would resort even to Satan himself, if necessary, to get sexual satisfaction.

Why was bromide once recommended for nineteenth-century American seamstresses?

To calm their sexual urges. Some doctors in the 1860s believed the rhythm of the sewing machine's treadle, or foot pedal, provoked sexual excitement in women. The bromide was thought to quell such urges. However, if improperly prescribed, it had the unfortunate side effect of doing away with the woman altogether.

Why were young Victorian women not allowed to hang up their boyfriend's picture?

Lest his eyes see her undress. The proscription usually applied just to the milady's bedroom. Victorian women were subject to a slew of mind-boggling strictures. In bed they were supposed to lay board still and not experience even the most ephemeral of passions. At least one prominent gynecologist of the time considered sexual desire in Victorian women to be pathological. Only whores felt pleasure.

Who once used dolls to tell the doctor where it hurt?

Victorian women. They would modestly point to that

doll part which corresponded to their own anatomy.

Who was Mrs. Grundy?

The morality watchdog of Victorian England. A personification of narrow-mindedness and social censure, Mrs. Grundy was born in Tom Morton's 1798 play, *Speed The Plow*.* Although her character never actually appeared on stage, the other actors were constantly evoking her presence with the incessant question, "What will Mrs. Grundy say?"

* Not to be confused with David Mamet's play of the same name.

What famous fictional character of the 1960s found his masturbatory pleasure in a pound of fresh liver?

Alexander Portnoy. *Portnoy's Complaint*, written by Phillip Roth in 1968, is riddled with the sexual fantasies, acting out and resultant guilt of its main character. The liver episode occurred during Portnoy's childhood and tells how he once commandeered a slab of liver from the family refrigerator and had his way with it. Racked with guilt for abusing his family's dinner, Portnoy washed the liver off and put it back into the fridge.

What notorious French writer sodomized chickens as well as anything or anyone else he could get his hands on?

The Marquis de Sade. Who else?

What erotic confectionary goods became very popular in the 1970s?

Cakes and tarts baked into the shape of intimate anatomical body parts.

Who wrote, "Marriage brings a man only two happy days: The day he takes his bride to bed, and the day he lays her in her grave"?

The Greek poet and likely misogynist, Palladas.

What famous actress was said to have sometimes slept in a coffin brimming over with love letters?

"The Divine Sarah." Sarah Bernhardt laid claim to over 1000 lovers in her lifetime and apparently relished rereading their letters in bed.

When was the first sex-change operation performed to turn a woman into a man?

In 1977. The new he was equipped with a hydraulic penis which could be pumped up when in the mood.

What world-famous shrine took 20,000 workers over 17 years to build and, when completed, was dedicated by a grieving husband to his eternally cherished wife?

The Taj Mahal, the most extravagant gift of love ever given. Mogul emperor Shah Jahan erected the beautiful, "jewel-like" building in Agra, India, in memory of his wife, Mumtaz Mahal (Exalted One of The Palace), after she died in childbirth in 1631. The Taj Majal has since come to symbolize one man's seemingly perfect love for and devotion to a woman.

What is the etymology of pornography?

Derived from the Greek word, *pornographos* (*porne* + prostitute + *graphein* + to write), *Webster's New World Dictionary* gives its original meaning as "writing about prostitutes."

Who did the first nude male centerfold in America?

Actor Burt Reynolds. It was the April, 1972 issue of *Cosmopolitan* that showed Burt with his hand sheepishly draped over his most private privates. Women loved the layout and Burt's career took off along with his clothes.

Why did Michelangelo's paintings on the ceiling of the Sistine Chapel come so dangerously close to being painted over?

Pope Paul IV considered the naked angels and several other nude figures in "The Last Judgment" indecent so he ordered them removed. An ensuing protest forced the Pope to rethink his position. Luckily, a compromise was soon reached and one of Michelangelo's students was commissioned to fix the offending figures by painting clothes on them.

Human sexual attraction may ultimately be explained by what skin emanation?

Phermones. It seems we all are endowed with a nose "sensor" that picks up odorless, chemical signals emanating from the skin of those to whom we are attracted. Phermones promise to explain why "love is blind" and why the most sane of us can fall hopelessly in love with a mutant.

What man made a fortune off the sexual philosophy, "Anything is permissible between consenting adults"?

Hugh Hefner - the man who built the Playboy empire.

What animal species not only mates face-to-face but apparently also has frequent sexual get-togethers to reduce social tension within the group?

The Bonobo Ape* of Zaire. It seems these apes use sex for more than just reproduction. They have a variety of gestures and vocalizations to let others in the group know when they are in the mood. It has been speculated that sex reduces tensions within the group and is one of the reasons why the bonobos can live together peacefully in relatively large numbers.

* The bonobo is the newest ape to be classified. Christened *Pan Paniscus* in 1930s, the bonobo is a cousin of the chimpanzee.

What was once referred to as the "French Disease"?

Syphilis. Not to be stuck with the rap, the French blamed it on the English, the English on the Spanish, and so on. Its origin was said to have been in the New World since it began spreading like wildfire throughout Europe right after Columbus's voyages to America.

Note: Experts now dispute this theory saying it is virtually impossible to know where syphilis actually originated. Bones revealing the evidence of syphilitic involvement have been found in different countries throughout the world dating back thousands of years. According to one Egyptologist, evidence of syphilis has been found in the skull of one of the workmen who helped build the pyramids 4,600 years ago.

What were the first condoms made from?

The bladders, intestines and organs of animals. These crude prophylactics date back hundreds, even thousands of years. There is some evidence suggesting that the Romans and Egyptians first used these pouchy prototypes. The rubber variety didn't come along until the 1870s when vulcanization was invented and the latex condom was born and streamlined.

What Greek philosopher thought love was "A grave mental disease"?

Plato.

Why did sweethearts, and even strangers, practice "bundling" in colonial America?

To keep warm. Purportedly because of a shortage of beds and inns in the colonies, strangers were allowed to sleep with a man's wife and/or daughters in order to stay warm. At least that was the pretext given for this strange hospitality custom that began early on in the American colonies and became widespread in the lower and middle-class rural areas from the 1750s to the 1780s. It was assumed, as a matter of honor, that everyone would keep their clothes on and behave. Apart from honor, a bundling board was sometimes placed in the middle of the bed to separate the familiar from the not-so-familiar bodies.

Note: Most historians don't buy into the notion that bundling was just about hospitality. They say it was basically a courtship ritual and it was in bed that young couples learned how to resist temptation. If they didn't and a pregnancy occurred, marriage quickly followed. Whatever the reasons for the custom, it quickly began to disappear as houses became better heated.

What made the Pussycat Theater in Los Angeles so famous in the early 1970s?

A porno film called *Deep Throat*, first released in 1972. Depicting the considerable fellatio talents of actress Linda Lovelace, the theater showed the film over 10 times a day for 10 years. Needless to say, the projector never got a chance to cool down.

Note: After Linda Lovelace retired from the not-so silver screen, she went on the lecture circuit as an anti-pornography spokesperson. Among other things, she spoke about how she had been forced into the porn business at gunpoint by her first husband. Though *Deep Throat* reportedly grossed some $600 million, Linda apparently never saw a penny of it.

What is comstockery?

The banning of books, art, plays, etc., deemed to be morally offensive and dangerous to public morals. The term was coined for Anthony Comstock (1844-1915), the self-appointed defender of American morality. Named by the U.S. Post Office as a "Special Agent" to watchdog and enforce the "Comstock Act," he went after just about everything he considered obscene - which was just about everything. Mr. Comstock passed his anti-vice mantle on to many present-day religious and political leaders who are still attempting to protect Americans from what they deem to be today's smut - which is just about everything.

Who believed diamonds were made from the fires of love?

The medieval Italians. That's why they preferred diamonds for their engagement rings. Made from the hardest of elements, diamonds would last forever - just like true love.

What is a "golden shower"?

Urinating on someone or being urinated on for sexual pleasure. The more proper term for this activity is *urolagnia*.

What 18th-century pornographic novel was involved in America's first obscenity case?

Fanny Hill, also known as *Memoirs of a Woman of Pleasure.* Penned by English writer John Cleland in 1749, American publisher Peter Holmes was arrested for printing it in the United States some 70 years later.* Deemed by many to be one of the most obscene books ever written, some of the novel's objectionable content included laughable euphemistic phrasings like: "the engine of love-assaults" (the penis); "delicious manuals of love devotion" (female breasts); "a just concert of springy heaves" (sexual intercourse); and, "his plenipotentiary instrument."

* Holmes was arrested for Fanny Hill's publication in 1821. It was not until 1963 that the United States finally lifted the ban on this novel and let Americans legally read it for the first time.

Who reportedly slept with naked women without ever having sex with them?

Gandhi. Some say he was testing his vow of celibacy.

What charming misanthrope once said, "My heart is a bargain today. Will you take it"?

W.C. Fields.

What vegetable has been called "testicle of the earth?"

The truffle. Considered a potent aphrodisiac, this expensive fungus is in a lot of "sexy" French cuisine.

What species of bird goes into a swooning free fall while mating in flight and regains consciousness but a few mere feet from the ground?

The swift.

What celebrity couple was said to have been caught having "table sex" at Ciro's, a famous Los Angeles nightclub on the Sunset Strip in the 1940s and 50s?

Paulette Goddard and movie director, Anatole Litvak. According to Allan Sherman's book, *The Rape of the APE (American Puritan Ethic)*, one or the other of them suddenly disappeared under the table during the floorshow and was soon caught in oral flagrante delicto by the management.

What revered Church icon and saint said, "Prostitution is a necessary condition of morality" and that "If you put down prostitution, license and pleasure will corrupt society"?

St. Augustine.

What was the "orgone box"?

A container about the size of a telephone booth that collected "orgasm energy" from the air. Invented in the 1940s by psychiatrist, Wilhelm Reich, the orgone box was an invaluable part of his therapy. A former student of Freud's, Reich thought the lack of orgasm was responsible for all his patient's health imbalances. To get well they had but to sit in his wooden, zinc-lined box and await their pleasure. If the universe's "orgasm energy" happened to be short on any given day, the good doctor is said to have pitched in and helped his patients out – whatever that was.

What famous French novelist observed, "Love is an art - the art of pleasing women"?

Honore Balzac (1799-1850). His book, *Physiologie du Mariage*, makes one surprising observation after another including, "One should never allow himself any pleasure with his wife unless he is first a master in the art of making her desire that same pleasure." This was surprising because pleasing women had never been a high priority among men in the Western world. But then, Balzac was full of a lot of surprises

What English king, who commissioned the authorized version of the English Bible, preferred the company of young men to his own queen?

King James I (r. 1603-25), the son of Mary Queen of Scots and the successor of Elizabeth I, he ruled over one of the most licentious courts in English history. He lavished small fortunes on the objects of his affection along with hereditary titles. One wonders if this randy sovereign ever had time to read the new *King James Version of The Bible* he commissioned.

What famous book of erotica refers to the male genitals as The Extinguisher of Passion, The Ransacker and The One-Eyed, among other colorful designations; and, to female genitalia as The Hedgehog, The Resigned and The Duellist?

The Perfumed Garden, written by fifteenth-century Tunisian scholar Shaykh Nefzawi and translated into English by Sir Richard Francis Burton in 1886.

Who was one of the first superstars to say "fuck" in a major motion picture?

Barbra Streisand. She uttered the expletive in the 1971 film, *The Owl and the Pussycat*.

Why did Southern Slav girls once roll pubic hair into cigarettes during the new moon?

The girls believed it would make the boys who smoked the cigarettes crazy about them.

What famous Queen's purported fellatio talents earned her the nickname *Meriochane,* "She who gapes wide for ten thousand men"?

Cleopatra, Egypt's last pharoah. Many scholars now agree that the awful nickname as well as the epithet, "Harlot Queen," were the inventions of her enemies, particularly the Romans, who greatly exaggerated the facts, especially anything that might cast Queen Cleopatra in a negative light.

What is a "courting stick" and how was it used in eighteenth-century America?

A hollowed-out, six-to-eight foot piece of wood, the courting stick was used by New England Puritans to safely separate a young couple and provide an acceptable way for them to communicate. In full view of their elders, the sweethearts were allowed to "whisper" through the stick to each other.

What is *The Ananga Ranga*?

The how-to-oriental-love-and-sex manual written by Indian author, Kalyana Malla, in the sixteenth century.

The *Ananga Ranga* has it all - love and seduction, sex and aphrodisiacs and, like *The Kama Sutra*, is illustrated with many different and very imaginative sexual positions. The book advises couples to constantly introduce new and exciting pleasures into their lovemaking in order to avoid boredom. The author says that the secret of a successful marriage is sexual spice. If one mixes it up with enough different positions, aphrodisiacs, etc., the variety will keep one's spouse eternally interested. Kalyana pointed out that such sexual diversity makes one's partner feel as if they are experiencing the pleasures of many different people instead of just one.

Why did the Church once recognize the missionary position as the only acceptable method of sexual intercourse?

All other positions were considered unnatural. Early theologians believed they either reversed the natural order of things (man on top) or interfered with conception.

Is the excuse, "I have a headache," a valid one for not having sex?

Supposedly not. Sex releases tension and relaxes the blood vessels in the brain. Therefore, the headache ought to disappear. Of course, if it's awful sex it could get a lot worse.

Who offered up the sentiment, "Thou art to me a delicious torment"?

American essayist and lecturer, Ralph Waldo Emerson.

After Lot flees Sodom and Gomorrah, what sexual sin did he commit for which other family members were blamed?

Incest. After his wife is turned to salt, he shacks up in a cave with his two daughters. They get Lot drunk and "bed" him so his "seed" would continue. The implication inherent in this Biblical tale is that since daddy was into his cups, his naughty daughters were at fault for the transgression. Why, then, is homosexuality associated with the fall of Sodom and Gomorrah and not incest as well?

What famous general and military genius took his male lover with him on many of his campaigns?

Alexander the Great. He also had a wife, possibly two. The one we know is Roxana.

Who is history's most famous polygamist?

King Solomon. The foxy old patriarch liked to seal political alliances with marriage and picked up 700 wives and 300 concubines along the way.

What sacred book contains the following passage as well as many other erotic tid-bits?

You are stately as a palm tree,
  and your breasts are like its clusters.
I say I will climb the palm tree
  and lay hold of its branches.
Oh, may your breasts be like
  clusters of the vine,
  and the scent of your breath like apples,
And your kisses like the best wine
  that goes down smoothly,
  gliding over lips and teeth ...

The Bible, the *Song of Solomon.*

Who so eloquently observed, "I love the love dealt out in kisses, bed and bread"?

Chilean poet, Pablo Neruda.

On what grounds did Pope Innocent III (1198-1216) allow the dissolution of marriage in the early thirteenth century?

Genital size. If a couple's genitals weren't a good fit and made sex difficult, dangerous or impossible, their marriage could be dissolved.

What writer of several best-selling pornographic books is also the well-known author of a series of horror novels?

Anne Rice. *Interview with the Vampire** is the most famous of her books in the popular series, *The Vampire Chronicles*. In another series, Anne penned the sadomasochistic likes of *The Claiming of Sleeping Beauty, Beauty's Punishment* and *Beauty's Release* under her alter ego, A.N. Roquelaure.

* Tom Cruise played the lead in the movie version of the book.

What tart-tongued observer of human nature once commented, "She's as pure as the driven slush"?

Tallulah Bankhead.

What erotic novel became a cultural phenomenon in 2011?

Fifty Shades of Grey by British writer E.L. James, the first of a very successful trilogy including *Fifty Shades Darker* and *Fifty Shades Freed*. The novels are graphic in their depiction of many sexual practices including sado-masochism and bondage. The series has reportedly bested even *Harry Potter* in sales. If true, any future installments of the latter may want to include a horny wizard.

What All-American, fresh-faced girl was pictured with a baby on the Ivory Snow laundry box in the 1970s before becoming a porn star?

Pure-as-a-drift-of-snow Marilyn Chambers. Her talent behind *The Green Door* (her first porn film) however, was the gig that brought her greater though more dubious fame.

How did the expression "Peeping Tom" reputedly come into being?

From legend. It refers to the English tailor who was struck blind after sneaking a "peep" at Lady Godiva as she rode naked astride a horse through Coventry. Today the epithet applies to anyone who gets his/her sexual kicks furtively leering at others through peepholes called windows.

What kind of falsie is a *braquette*?

A leather penile sheath worn in the late Middle Ages.

What international playboy of the 1940s and 50s had the nickname, "Always Ready"?

Porfirio Rubirosa. His unfailing and ever-ready amorous talents seduced a whole host of women into marriage including Barbara Hutton, the F.W. Woolworth heiress; Doris Duke, the Reynolds tobacco heiress; and, Flor Trujillo, the daughter of Dominican Republic dictator Generalissimo Rafael Trujillo. Zsa Zsa Gabor, Veronica Lake, Marilyn Monroe, Kim Novak and Delores Del Rio were also persuaded by his charms but chose not to take a walk down the aisle with him.

Note: Rubirosa had an Italian pepper grinder named after him. Apparently the size and shape of the "rubirosa" resembled an unforgettable part of the playboy's anatomy.

What are supernumerary nipples?

More than two nipples. The phenomenon is not as rare as one might think and even men may sport an extra nipple or two, neatly aligned one below the other. One account in a medical magazine from the late 1900s tells of a young woman with nine breasts, seven of which reportedly gave milk.

When were vibrators first electrified?

At the beginning of the 1900s. These electrical miracles weren't cheap. One of them, christened the "Chattanooga," was available only by mail order and cost a couple of hundred dollars plus shipping.

Note: The vibrator was invented in the 1880s and originally operated like a wind-up toy - no doubt winding down just as milady reached critical mass.

What erudite 19th-century English writer and scholar was said to have been stunned into abstinence at the sight of his wife's pubic hair on their wedding night?

John Ruskin. Some biographers claim he died a virgin and that his latent homosexuality was probably the cause of his abstinence. Notwithstanding his sexual repression or, perhaps, because of it, Ruskin's literary output was prodigious. For starters, he wrote a five-volume treatise on art called *Modern Painters* which he followed up with *The Seven Lamps of Architecture* and his famous tome, *The Stones of Venice*.

What is sexsomnia?

Sleep sex. The sexsomniac may engage in a variety of sex activities while still asleep including masturbation, fondling his/herself and even having sex with another person. Many things can trigger the condition including but not limited to stress, insomnia, the excessive use of alcohol and/or drugs, etc. The sexsomniac is said not to remember the sex they have while asleep.

Why do some people, mostly men, engage in the practice of autoerotic asphyxiation?

To heighten orgasm. Hundreds of men reportedly die each year while choking off the air supply to their brains in an attempt to induce "the big one."

What sexual rite of passage is performed on pubescent girls in India and many developing countries of Africa and Asia?

A cliterodectomy. The clitoris of young girls is excised thinking it will keep them chaste and faithful to their future husbands. In fact, most men where this custom is observed won't marry a female with an intact clitoris. Female mutilation, it appears, is the price paid in some parts of the world to assuage the male ego's fear of losing control over women. A more radical procedure called infibulation is also popular in many of the same parts of the world. In this case, except for a small opening left for urination, a woman's vagina (the labia) is sewn completely shut to prevent sexual intercourse until marriage.

Note: Many organizations are now educating men and women in an effort to end female mutilation wherever it is practiced in the world.

What perennial playboy unabashedly admits he uses Viagra?

Hugh Hefner. He claims it's a great recreational drug.

What highly educated, renowned French courtesan practiced her profession well into her sixties and was said to have been the lover to three generations of men from the same family?

Ninon de Lenclos (1616-1705). Unrivalled in her many talents as a lady of love, Ninon found time for other pursuits as well. Notably, she established a very famous "love school" that both men and women attended. They were given expert advice on such subjects as the ABCs of seduction, the physiology of sex, the art of romance, the psychology of men and women, how to treat a mistress, how to end an affair, etc. Almost 90 when she died, she had the respect of men and women equally in the upper reaches of French society. She charmed everyone.

Involuntary contractions, or spasms, of the vagina may result in what painful predicament?

Vaginismus. Anxiety or a sudden fright may trigger the condition. If a woman is having intercourse when it occurs, the penis may be locked into a vaginal spasm from which it cannot easily escape. One famous incident occurred in France at the end of the nineteenth century when President Francois Faure suddenly died while having sex in a bordello. His untimely expiration so scared milady that her vagina begin to spasm uncontrollably and clamped down on the President's penis so hard, as the story goes, that it had to be surgically removed.

Did Catherine the Great, Empress of Russia, really die in one final act of bestiality?

Rumors about the Empress have been running amok ever since she died at the end of the eighteenth century. Some sources say the rumors aren't rumors at all - that Catherine expired while "consorting with" a horse. Others say neigh, sheer rubbish - she died of a cerebral hemorrhage. Reputable historians agree, the stories are pure fiction.

What famous romantic poet waxed, "As in the soft and sweet eclipse when soul meets soul on lover's lips"?

Percy Bysshe Shelley, the husband of *Frankenstein* author, Mary Shelley.

What nineteenth-century performer renowned for her awful "tarantella," or spider dance, and fiery temper, attracted a long list of very notable men, all of whom she took as lovers?

Lola Montez. Born Eliza Gilbert in Ireland, tales of Lola's charms quickly spread to the continent where she took up with the likes of Alexandre Dumas, Ludwig I of Bavaria, Victor Hugo, Captain James and Franz Liszt just to mention a paltry few. Her attraction was magnetic.

According to some, she was heaven and hell rolled into one. Easily angered, chaos preceded and followed Lola wherever she went, earning her the not-so-endearing epithet of "Apocalyptic Whore." Could she be the source of the saying, "Whatever Lola wants, Lola gets"?

Why is it almost impossible to tell a female from a male spotted hyena?

Their sexual organs are virtually identical. The clitoris of the female is elongated and enlarged to resemble the size and shape of the male penis. Her organ can become erect like the males and her fused labia resemble a scrotum. So close are the similarities between them that only an expert can tell them apart, usually by palpating their scrotums.

Who was arrested in 1951 simply for taking a bubble bath?

Stripper Lili St. Cyr. It seems the glass bathtub she used on stage contained far more water than bubbles. While the audience at Ciro's nightclub in Los Angeles was delighted to view Lili's bare assets, LA's vice squad didn't share their sentiment and carted Lili off to jail.

Who said, "A cigar is sometimes just a cigar"?

Sigmund Freud. In other words, even in the heavily laden symbolic world of the sexual unconscious, Freud himself admitted that a cigar was not always a phallic symbol but sometimes just a plain old cigar.

What famous English writer and poet undoubtedly waxed his true sentiments when he wrote, "A woman is only a woman, but a good cigar is a smoke"?

Rudyard Kipling. Maybe he and Freud should have gotten together and compared cigars.

Who thoughtfully observed, "It isn't premarital sex if you have no intention of getting married"?

Drew Carey.

What infamous officer of German's Third Reich was an unlikely but very successful seducer of women?

Hitler's evil propaganda genius, Joseph Goebbels. He was only a little over five feet tall, walked with a limp and had a face like a weasel. His deficits, however, do not appear to have been off-putting with women. Obsessed with sex and a notorious ladies man, Goebbels was nicknamed "the ram" by the countless ones he seduced.

How did Leah, in *The Book of Genesis*, win back Jacob's love and get him to sleep with her again?

By giving him an aphrodisiac called mandrake. Leah's success resulted in Jacob's fifth son. The plant, vaguely resembling the shape of a human being, was believed to be a love potion in Biblical times and is still used in some parts of the world for that same purpose today.

What ancient civilization believed that rotting fish entrails were an exquisite aphrodisiac?

The Romans.

What eccentric billionaire/director designed a bra to fit his leading lady in the early 1940s film, *The Outlaw*?

Howard Hughes. The brassiere was created for the picture's star, Jane Russell, and Hughes made sure the leading lady's leading assets were prominently featured whenever possible.

<u>Note</u>: Though Hughes was given credit as the film's director, Howard Hawks actually did most of the directing.

What was sexy actress Terry Moore said to be wearing beneath her clothes when she appeared at a Korean army base show in 1953?

An ermine bathing suit. The soldiers who attended the show claim they didn't see any bathing suit. Their cheers, however, apparently attested to what they thought they did see. Obviously the guys had been in Korea a tad too long – their imaginations were working in overdrive.

Are "virgin births" possible?

Yes. *Parthenogenesis** or unisexual reproduction, as it is scientifically referred to, is not infrequent among some insects. It takes place when the female's egg reproduces without having been fertilized by a male's sperm.

* *Parthenos* (virgin or maiden) + *genesis* (generation).

What kind of love is *Teufelbuhlschaft*?

"Devil's love." Sexual attraction to and copulation with the devil has figured in Church literature for a long time as one of the "sins of complete lechery."

Who once mused, "I never quite understood it - this sex symbol… But if I'm going to be a symbol of something, I'd rather have it be sex than some of the other things they've got symbols for"?

Marilyn Monroe.

What lexical designation regarding sexual preference is not found in Hindi, the official language of India?

Lesbian. In the 1997 Indian-made film, *Fire*, two women lovingly point this out. Their language simply has no word to describe what they are.

How did cynic and literary wit, H.L. Mencken, sum up love?

As "...a state of perceptual anesthesia."

Who invented the bra?

Not a man as is commonly believed. It was actually designed by a New York socialite named Mary Phelps Jacob in 1913 – at least she was the one who received a patent for it. It was a case of the old adage, "necessity being the mother of invention," that inspired Mary to come up with the bra. A particular gown she wanted to wear to a social event that evening revealed the whalebone in her corset, the undergarment worn at the time. She needed something that would give her support but wouldn't poke through the sheer fabric of the dress she planned to wear. She improvised with two silk handkerchiefs and some ribbon - then voila´, the prototype of the brassiere came into being.

What married Victorian poets supposedly never saw each other completely nude?

Robert and Elizabeth Barrett Browning. Considering the uptightness that characterizes the Victorian era, such is possible. Many Victorian women confessed that they had never seen a totally naked man in their life. In fact, one woman reportedly told English psychologist Havelock Ellis (*Studies in the Psychology of Sex*) that even though she had borne her husband several children, she had no idea what his body looked like.

What Victorian wit, playwright and poet penned the following cynical observation about love?

Yet each man kills the thing he loves,
By each let this be heard,
Some do it with a bitter look,
Some with a flattering word,
The coward does it with a kiss,
The brave man with a sword!

Oscar Wilde. The verse is only one of several such verses from his poetic masterpiece, *The Ballad of Reading Gaol*. Wilde wrote it shortly after he got out of jail for homosexuality.

Who wrote a book about a man who so wanted to be a woman that he had his penis removed only to realize "he" was actually a lesbian?

Gore Vidal. His 1968 novel, *Myra Breckinridge*, titillated everyone and led to a 1970 film by the same name starring Racquel Welch.

What newspaper publisher had a poster designed in the 1960s that featured Disney cartoon characters engaging in objectionable activities?

Paul Krassner of the 1960s underground newspaper, *The Realist*. Krassner "commissioned" a poster in 1965 that showed Mickey and Minnie, Donald and Pluto, Snow White and the Seven Dwarfs all occupied in an inventive array of sex acts with each other. One can only imagine the comic possibilities.

What's the difference between an incubus and a succubus?

An incubus is a medieval demon, or spirit, that sneaked into the beds of sleeping women and had sexual intercourse with them. A succubus did the same thing, only with guys.

What was the purpose of the Kama Shastra Society?

Founded by Sir Richard Francis Burton and Foster Fitzgerald Arbuthnot, the Society dedicated itself to the publication of rare works of erotic Oriental literature. *The Kama Sutra, The Perfumed Garden* and *The Ananga Ranga* were three of the titles* they chose to publish privately. Why privately? Full of adventurous sexual positions, recipes for aphrodisiacs, etc., the books would have shocked the socks off the average Victorian who could barely manage the missionary, man-on-top sexual position. Remember, these were the days when people believed that really decent women didn't enjoy sex and thought of those who did as whores.

* The first two were translated by Burton and the third by both Burton & Arbuthnot.

How did the "XXXs" lovers so often use to represent kisses purportedly originate?

In early Christian times a cross mark, or an "X," was used as a signature by people who didn't know how to sign their names to legal documents. It became customary to kiss the "X mark" afterwards to show the signer's total sincerity. This custom morphed into the "X" being associated with a lover's kiss and its use in sweet missives.

What 1960s underground newspaper, usually credited with being America's first, printed anything and everything fit or not fit to be read?

The Los Angeles Free Press. When its first issue appeared on the stands in July of 1964, Angelenos began reading about things they might have once only imagined. Nothing was off limits anymore. The words, pictures, stories and ads appearing in *The LA Free Press* alternately amused, shocked and outraged its readership. There was no denying it. The sexual revolution was here to stay and all the salacious details could now be savored in black and white.

Where did the words, "*Si Non Oscillas, Noli Tintinnare* - If you don't swing, don't ring," originally appear?

The plaque appeared below the doorbell to Hugh Hefner's private apartment on the second floor of the Chicago Playboy Mansion. The words are also said to be visible on the front of Hefner's Holmby Hills mansion in Los Angeles.

Who wrote the 1969 best-selling smut novel, *Naked Came a Stranger*?

Penelope Ashe, the nom de plume for fifteen different writers who each penned one of the book's chapters. All members of Long Island's *Newsday* staff, everyone had agreed to write the raciest stuff they could imagine. And so they did. That their collective inspiration inspired the high number of book sales it did speaks volumes about America's collective taste for the prurient, even back then.

Did Beethoven's Immortal Beloved really exist?

A movie by the same name released in 1994 with Gary Oldman is based on the premise that she did. Fueling the controversy is a letter Beethoven purportedly wrote to his "Immortal Beloved" found in a secret desk drawer after he died. Whether the letter is the copy of one Beethoven actually sent his secret beloved or just a desperate fantasy remains a mystery. The letter commanded an actual or imaginary love to "...continue to love me, never misjudge the faithful heart of your beloved L. - Ever yours - Ever mine - Ever each other's."

In what popular Renaissance book does the following exhortation appear, "Women are repulsive to the touch? In intercourse, they are deadly dangerous. The man who lies with them seeks death"?

Malleus Maleficarum. The book became the Church's definitive witch-hunting manual beginning in the 1480s and reminded so for the next two centuries. Written by the Dominican monks, Kramer and Sprenger, it tells in painstaking detail how to recognize a witch, catch her and kill her. A misogynistic blueprint without peer, hundreds of thousands of women (some accounts say millions) were burned at the stake, drowned, tortured to death, beheaded, or otherwise fatally dispatched. Almost anything made a woman suspect - a mole on her body, freckles, the belief she filched semen from sleeping men, not drowning when tossed into water, etc. Such "evidence" more than earned the perpetrator a quick "trial" and an instant ticket to hell.

What 1970's film immortalized the often-spoofed line, "Love is never having to say you're sorry"?

Love Story starring Ryan O'Neal and Ali MacGraw. The film was a rather literal rendition of Erich Segal's sappy, best-selling novel by the same name.

What famous town in 17ᵗʰ-century France blamed its nuns' sexual fantasies on the devil?

Loudon. It seems the Ursuline nuns living there in 1634 were either being romanced by devils or suffering from mass hysteria. It all started when Mother Superior Jeanne des Anges began making suggestive pelvic motions and cavorting about the convent proclaiming Iscaacaron, a lusty devil, was having at her. The other nuns quickly got into the act moaning wantonly and gyrating their pelvises as well. One even suffered a false pregnancy. The matter was ultimately resolved when the Church's best exorcists sent the pesky devils packing. Aldous Huxley chronicled the events at Loudon in his book, *The Devils of Loudon*, and Ken Russell treated the world to a cinemagraphic version of the events in his film, *The Devils*.

What event is said to mark the beginning of the gay liberation movement?

The Stonewall Riots of June 27, 1969. A routine police raid of a gay bar in Greenwich Village ignited a riot when the homosexuals they were arresting finally got tired of being harassed. The Stonewall Inn was torched and the rioting spread, lasting throughout the night and into the weekend. Within a few weeks lesbians and gays organized themselves and the gay liberation movement was born.

Why is it that Jews have historically considered male homosexuality a more serious offense than lesbianism?

The most popular interpretation suggests that since the male variety "wastes the seed," it was more offensive to God. Semen is/was considered a sacred fluid and squandering it, an unthinkable transgression. Mose Maimonides, a rabbi who lived during the twelfth century, supposedly went so far as to say lesbianism wasn't so bad. There was no seed wasting.

What happens to the male box turtle if the female gets tired of mating with him?

She closes her shell and castrates him. In order to avoid such a calamity the smart male sticks his foot under the female's shell while mating. Apparently, this part of the male box turtle's anatomy can more successfully cope with any sudden changes in the female's mood.

Who considered the delaying of male orgasm an art?

The Arabs. *Imsak*, as Sir Richard Burton noted in his translation of the *Arabian Nights*, was the, practice of delaying sexual gratification. Those men who became proficient at *Ismak* were able to distract their minds while relaxing certain overly tense muscles. The ability made them highly coveted as lovers.

Note: The Chinese and Indians also make reference to such a practice at different times in their history. Western man, however, has few references to such a practice. It's why Hindu women once referred to Europeans as "village-cocks." Other than a lot of strut and cock-a-doodle-do, they thought most Western men had little to offer in bed except the same old, unimaginative stuff.

How long would it theoretically take one man's sperm to populate the United States?

Three days according to one account. A healthy pair of testicles produces some 72 million sperm a day. It's all in how you crunch the numbers. Go figure.

What is one of the recommended cures for lesbianism?

Cauterization or cutting off the clitoris. At least that was the spiritual counsel Piscetta and Gennaro gave in their 1940 book, *Elements of Theological Morals.*

Who said, "Everyone ends up kissing the wrong person good night"?

Andy Warhol.

What former kindergarten teacher and charmingly blunt grandmother became television's most popular, celebrity sex therapist during the 1970s and 1980s?

Dr. Ruth Westheimer. Always at the ready when it came to dispensing frank sexual advice, Dr. Ruth appeared on every TV show you can think of and made even the hosts blush at the straightforward, humorous and unselfconscious way she talked about sex. Between shows she penned several best-selling books including *Dr. Ruth's Guide to Good Sex* and *The Art of Arousal*. She also created a board game and eventually hosted "Good Sex," her own television show. Sex is one of life's true blessings, Dr. Ruth told the world, people should stop being so uptight about it.

What remedy is suggested in Shaykh Nefzawi's book, *The Perfumed Garden*, for enlarging a small penis?

Among the suggestions Nefzawi makes to help "insignficant members," or ones that are "soft, nerveless and relaxed," is to rub them with tepid water. This will make the timid member less timid, more energetic, and extended as blood rushes through it. Nefzawi also recommends vigorously massaging a mixture of ginger and honey into the hopefully, by now, tumescent member.

Note: Since this is a rather ancient remedy, it might not be wise to actually put it to the test. Ginger can burn like a son of a gun and honey might not put out the fire.

What unusual commodity did a young woman called Natalie Dylan succeed in auctioning off on the internet in 2009?

Her purported virginity - how it would have been objectively confirmed, however, isn't clear. In any event, the highest bidder offered her 3.8 million for first time privileges then backed out. Natalie reportedly kept his hefty deposit and supposedly went on to ink a book deal about bartering with her maidenhead.

When was the notion of "romantic love" introduced to the world?

Many scholars say it began during the 1100s in southern France with Eleanor of Aquitaine's "Courts of Love." While her husband, Henry II, went across the Channel to claim the English throne, Eleanor stayed behind in Aquitaine for a while and presided over a court that welcomed troubadours and poets who wrote about love. The Courts of Love stressed the radical new notion of mutuality in love relationships between men and women rather than those of necessity and expediency, or master and servant. Throwing off the yoke of history, however, was not so easy. Women were men's property. To try to ignore or get around this, chivalry and idealized love were born. It became fashionable to love someone from afar and let the "lady love" know about one's heart through verse or song. Sometimes, however, lovers (frequently married) proved unable to love from afar and risked everything for an adulterous liaison such as did Guinevere and Lancelot. The ultimate legacy of Courtly Love, claim some scholars, is not really about love at all but rather about pain and suffering. To wit, writer Francois duc de La Rochefoucauld noted in the 1600s that "people would never fall in love if they had not heard love talked about." In other words, he believed as many others did, that love was nothing more than a medieval invention.

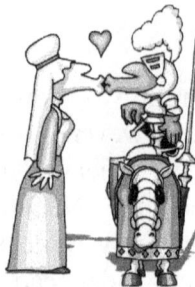

The Instant Voyeur

What do the French call crab lice?

Papillons d'amour - butterflies of love. Leave it to the French to poeticize these unpleasant little buggers.

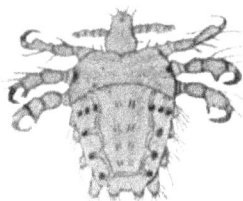

Note: *Pediculosis pubis*, or crab lice, is not just acquired from sexual contact but also from more casual contact such as with contaminated bedclothes.

When 16th-century monarch is said to have been one of the first women to start wearing "panties"?

As the story goes, Catherine de Medici, the wife of Henri II of France, was riding a horse one day when a gust of wind blew her skirts up and revealed God's all to her husband's court. Since only the men wore underwear then, Catherine decided to appropriate their *calcons* for her very own. Apparently, the men weren't pleased. They wanted women to remain just as bare bottomed as they had been born. Besides, to their way of thinking, skirts provided all the modesty any lady ever really needed until, of course, a big wind blew in.

In England what does "shagging" or "rogering" mean?

Exactly what you're thinking it does. But if you have any doubt just see an *Austin Powers'* movie.

91

What book, written in the fourteenth century, recounts the lusty storytelling of a group of people who fled Florence to escape the Bubonic Plague?

The Decameron. Considered a masterpiece of world literature, this book by Boccaccio describes how seven women and three men hold up in a villa outside Florence for ten days and tell each other stories. By turns romantic and ribald, picaresque and shocking, the storytelling diverts the group from the horror in nearby Florence where the "Black Death" is claiming one out of every four people.

What two forms of love are polar opposites?

Eros is the carnal variety and agape, the spiritual sort.

What eighteenth-century actress and author can boast nearly as many, if not as many, sexual conquests as Casanova?

Mille DuBois. She is said to have once catalogued the number of lovers she had over a 20 year period and the count came to 16,525 or so (let's not quibble), averaging over two assignations a day.

Why would a dead man's sperm be salvaged?

To impregnate a female. A procedure called "post-mortem sperm retrieval" was successfully used in 1998 to retrieve the sperm of a man who had been dead for 30 hours because his widow decided she wanted to have his child. Experts think the sperm was still viable because the man's body had been put into cold storage almost immediately upon his expiration.

How old was the oldest woman to ever marry?

The distinction belongs to Minnie Munro of Australia who tied the knot when she was 102 years young. Minnie wed Mr. Dudley Reid who was but a mere 83 years of age at the time of their nuptials.

What military genius reportedly had an abnormally small penis?

Napoleon. Some say it measured no more than an inch. Others swear it was the length of a small finger. Whatever the case, an American urologist purchased Napoleon's penis in the late 1970s for close to four thousand dollars.

What clothing did the Church encourage women to wear in the Middle Ages that was meant to reduce their sexual pleasure?

The *chemise cagoule*. Since the Church considered sex a necessary evil to be used only for procreation, this heavy woolen nightshirt with a precision-cut hole in the front afforded little pleasure for the would-be procreators, especially the women.

How many people in the United States reportedly have a STD or a sexually transmitted disease?

According to one account, about 20%. But like all statistics, it depends on how the numbers are crunched. Could be less, could be more. The number of different STDs bedeviling Americans is said to be in excess of a dozen including syphilis, gonorrhea, genital herpes, genital warts, chlamydiosis, proctitis, chancoid, nonspecific urethritis, balanoposthitis, etc. A whole slew of bacterial pathogens can also be transmitted sexually, including shigella, campylobacteria and salmonella, as well as parasitic organisms like giardiasis and amebiasis. Who could have guessed there were so many viral, bacterial and parasitic sexual predators out there.

If a Puritan woman in the early American colonies committed adultery and refused to wear the big "A" on the front of her dress, what might the elders then do to her?

Permanently brand the letter "A"on her face.

What is venereophobia?

Fear of venereal disease, usually abnormally so.

A nympholeptic suffers from what?

An obsessive storm of erotic emotion, a frenzied ecstasy if you will, for something or someone they cannot have or ever attain.

Before penicillin came along, how was syphilis treated?

With mercury and arsenic. The treatment was greatly feared because it could be as bad as the disease itself, or worse. While many who took mercury and arsenic were cured of syphilis, many of them also spent the rest of their lives in chronic bad health.

Note: The use of heavy metals (mercury, arsenic and bismuth preparations) to treat syphilis began in the late 1400s and remained unchanged as the therapy of choice until penicillin came along at the end of World War II.

Other than being used as a seasoning for certain dishes, what romantic use does the bay leaf have on the night of February 14th?

According to sources, mostly gypsies, the bay leaf will inspire dreams of one's true love if placed under the dreamer's pillow.

***Girls' Dormitory, Sin, Duet in Darkness, Satan's Daughter,* and *Odd Girl Out* are all titles of what genre paperback original appearing in the 1950s?**

The lesbian dime store novel. During that decade bookracks spilled over with paperbacks bearing titillating covers of women touching and looking at each other suggestively. Inside were sizzling tales of forbidden love and passionate trysts. Considering the times, it's hard to believe this kind of novel ever made it into print much less into stores. One possible explanation is that few, if any, of these books had a happy ending. Retribution always came in one form or another. The protagonists were either discovered and forced apart or died in some terrible accident. The message was simple: lesbians were not allowed to be happy - at least not in the fifties.

Who analyzed that maddening dynamic between lovers as, "Where they love they do not desire and where they desire they do not love"?

Sigmund Freud.

What did the sexual manual, *Aristotle's Master-piece*, published in England in the 17th century, propose for milady's foreplay pleasure?

A very light clitoral stroking. By "blowing the coals of these amorous fires," it assured male readers, women would soon become passionately receptive.

Who said, "Americans make love worse than any other race on earth"?

Poet-essayist-journalist-writer Walt Whitman. The quote appeared in his 1862 book, *An American Primer*. Whitman achieved international renown for his collection of poems, *Leaves of Grass*, first published in 1855.

To what did "nose art" refer during World War II?

The female nudes painted on the noses of Navy fighter planes. Such "art" was sanctioned by the U.S. Navy itself because it boosted spirits and help reinforce "healthy" heterosexual fantasies in the sex-segregated military.

What were the first erotic books printed in America called?

"Satanic Literature." Irish surgeon William Haynes invested the money he made from publishing the pornographic import, *Fanny Hill*, into a very successful line of cheap erotica. In the 1850s his books were soon appearing just about everywhere in America and even became a "barracks favorites" during the Civil War. In spite of all the hell-and-damnation warnings, the devil's literature couldn't have been more popular.

What famous poet, husband of an equally famous poet-wife sentimentalized, "Grow old along with me! The best is yet to be"?

Robert Browning. This quote often appears etched on sundials.

Besides inventing "Corn Flakes," what enterprising health venture helped make Dr. John Harvey Kellogg famous at the turn of the century?

A sanitarium, or "health spa," he ran in Battle Creek, Michigan. The cures at the Battle Creek Sanitarium were directed at curbing sexual appetites and extinguishing the urge to masturbate. Dr. Kellogg considered the former an abomination and the latter, a sure path to a whole host of diseases including tuberculosis and leprosy. Idiocy also figured high on his list of possible afflictions. Dr. Kellogg's "Sanitas Corn Flakes," as they were originally called, along with various other bland foods served at the spa supposedly helped cure his patients of their beastly appetites. *The Road to Wellville*, a 1994 movie starring Anthony Hopkins, recounts Kellogg's near religious fanaticism in both sexual and health matters.

Who was supposedly the inspiration for the Country & Western classic, "The Yellow Rose of Texas"?

A whore from Galveston. But just and try to get a Texan to agree with you.

How did the fellows in the Roman Court take an oath?

They swore on their testicles. Instead of raising their hand, they supposedly grasped their scrotum with one hand and pledged the oath they were taking with the other. To wit, a present-day lawyerly source points to the etymology of testify as being derived from testis or testes. Not much of a case for the tale's veracity but a good story nonetheless.

What is variocele?

Not Italian pasta but varicose veins of the testicles. The condition reportedly affects upwards of 10 percent of all men.

The mores of what historical era compelled proper folk to reserve separate shelves in their libraries for those books written by male and female authors?

The Victorian. Propriety demanded it and absurdity quickly obliged. How such male/female proximity in the inanimate world invited trouble is difficult to fathom but the Victorians always seemed to be able to accommodate even the most unfathomable rationales.

What shocking solution did a Baptist minister propose for extinguishing homosexuality?

Charles Worley, Pastor of Providential Baptist Church in Maiden, N.C., told his flock on May 13, 2012, that lesbians should be flung behind one electrified fence and all the men "queers" behind another until they died out. Meanwhile, he added, planes could fly over and do food drops. For some reason he stopped just short of asking Jehovah to pelt the bunch with fire-and-brimstone before they even got to hell. The Pastor's outrageous sermon instantly went viral on YouTube.

What is amplexus?

Amphibian sex. It's the scientific term used to designate intercourse between frogs, toads, newts, etc.

Sylvester Graham (1794-1851), the inventor of the graham cracker, believed what non-culinary activity shortened one's life?

Sexual overindulgence. This was especially true for men since Graham thought each ejaculation lowered a man's life expectancy.

Which century's "secret societies" were devoted almost exclusively to the pursuit of pleasure?

The eighteenth century. The lustful battle cry of the times was best summed up by the French "*libertinage de la pensee*" or, the licentiousness of thought. Private salons sprang up throughout Paris celebrating every conceivable erotic pursuit as did clubs in England. Debauchery reigned even among the royals. Philip of Orleans, the Regent of France, supposedly headed up one of these secret circles and indulged himself in ever more exotic ways to satisfy his increasingly dissipated self.

SECRET

Note: One secret society, or sect, was called the "Multiplicants." Members of this group met clandestinely, married, and then consummated their unions before three witnesses. Twenty-four hours later the couples were no longer bound by their vows and could actively seek out other partners.

Women of what Amazonian tribe spit into a man's face as a greeting or to show their affection for him?

The Chorowti. The women are also said to spit into the man's face during intercourse to show their pleasure.

When did the first successful artificial insemination in history supposedly take place?

In 1782. Dr. John Hunter, a London doctor, retrieved semen from a man with *hypospadias** who he had told to masturbate. The doctor then injected the semen into the man's wife and nine months later she gave birth.

* A congenital abnormality of the penis in which the urethral opening is located on the underside of that organ. In the case cited the condition prevented the man's sperm from efficiently exiting his penis during sex and making a successful trip up the vaginal canal to impregnate his wife.

How did the honeymoon custom begin?

With abduction, at least that's one of the explanations. In Northern Europe scads of years ago when the number of women in a given village got too low, a man would just go steal one from another village. In order to avoid being caught by the woman's family, the couple would go into hiding until the search for her was called off. The time they spent together, or "honeymoon," was supposedly derived from an ancient Norse word that meant hiding. A more popular explanation for the origin of honeymoon centers on the custom of drinking a cup of mead, or honeyed wine, during the first month, or one cycle of the moon, that a married couple spends together.

If you are *"frottaging"* someone, what are you doing to them?

Rubbing your genitals up against them, usually in a crowd. People who have this condition (*frottage*, from Fr., rubbing) have a highly revved-up libido that induces an overpowering and frequently uncontrollable impulse to press up against someone in hopes of producing an orgasm.

Note: *Frottage* is also a massage technique.

What Nobel Prize-winning author was one of the first influential people of the twentieth century to defend homosexuality as well as publicly assert his own?

Andre Gide (1869-1951). *Corydon*, his defense of homosexuality published in 1924, caused such a public uproar that Gide left France and moved to Africa for a while. While there he exposed colonial abuse in his 1927 *Travels in the Congo*.

If you are into *algolagnia*, what are you into?

One side or the other of the S&M equation, or both. The dictionary defines *algolagnia* as the aberrant sexual pleasure derived from inflicting or suffering pain.

What fairy tale character asked, "Do you love me because I am beautiful, or am I beautiful because you love me"?

Cinderella.

What Shakespearean character descends into madness and drowns herself after being dumped by the man she loves?

Ophelia.   Her madness and suicide are inextricably bound to her feelings of deception and rejection by Hamlet and a series of tragic events, including the death of her father.   Scholars may take exception at such a facile explanation since most all the characters in *Hamlet* are extremely complex.   That said, character motives and motivations in *Hamlet* can be argued until the cows come home and still not satisfy everyone.

> Hamlet: *I did love you once.*
> Ophelia: *Indeed, my, lord, you made me believe so.*
> Hamlet: *You should not have believed me...I loved you not.*
> Ophelia: *I was the more deceived.*

When do half of all injuries to the penis supposedly occur?

During sex, specifically during intercourse.

After two land snails mate, why can they both lay eggs?

They're hermaphrodites.

What is the difference between *zoophilism*, *zoolagnia* and *zooerasty*?

The first is an abnormal love of animals. The second

is a strong sexual desire for animals. The third is sexual intercourse with animals, or bestiality.

What does the term ithyphallic mean?

An erect penis. Archaeologists use the word to denote the phalli seen in old murals, paintings and statues. In particular, the term is applied when referring to the Egyptian fertility god, Min, depicted here with no add-on.

Shakespeare used the image of "the beast with two backs" to conjure up what in *Othello*?

Sexual intercourse.

What ancient Indian medical text stated that a woman would bear a child resembling that person she thought about during conception?

Charaka Samita. Apparently, Hindu texts weren't the only ones that referred to such a belief. The writings of the ancient Greeks did as well. For them fantasy and imagination played a powerful role in determining the physical and mental attributes of offspring.

What are Exposed Gills, Mandarin Ducks and Winding Dragon?

If you guessed some noveau Chinese cuisine, you're wrong. The terms actually refer to a few of the imaginative and varied sexual positions listed in Master Tung-Hsuang's seventh-century love-and-sex book, *Ars Amatoria**. Some other descriptive possibilities include: Bamboos by the Altar and the Cleaving Cicada, Gamboling Wild Horses, Firm Attachment and Phoenix Sporting in the Cinnabar Cleft.

* Not to be confused with Ovid's love manual, *Ars Amatoria*.

What aquatic creature can change its sex back and forth between male and female?

A goby, specifically the *Gobiodon histrio* species, found in certain coral areas off Australia's Great Barrier Reef. Apparently, as the demand rises within the mating population, males can change into females if more of the latter are needed to propagate the species.

What southern state made voyeurism an exclusively male crime in 1958?

Mississippi. Apparently women down there have never been as interested as men in taking a sneaky peek at others. At least that's what the state legislators figured when they passed the law. But who knows? Maybe those southern belles just know how not to get caught or they were good lobbyists.

What virile animal, symbol of muscle, power and money cannot sustain an erection for more than 30 seconds?

The bull. At least it's said he can't manage to mate much longer than that.

What popular animated television character was accused of being a homosexual in 1999?

Tinky Winky of the Teletubbies. The guy's little purple outfit, headgear and purse apparently made him suspect with America's religious right. Reverend Jerry Falwell, among others, voiced concern about Tinky Winky's tendencies on national television. As a result, the little guy became more popular than ever.

What famous American writer was said to have created pornography when he published *1601* in 1888?

Mark Twain. Critic Edward Wagenknecht described Twain's *1601* as "the most famous piece of pornography in American literature." While the work may be risqué it is hardly obscene, just colorful. Twain himself often said of the book, "If there's a decent word in it, it is because I overlooked it."

"Playing the flute" referred to what sexual activity in ancient Greece?

Fellatio.

Who dreamily remarked after repeatedly trysting with the President of the United States in the Oval Office that they were "sexual soul mates"?

Monica Lewinsky. The "sexual soul mate" to which she referred was, of course, Bill Clinton. Soul considerations aside, Monica and Bill were apparently also very successful sexual phone mates.

What form of sex can is said to provide its practitioners with multiple orgasms as well as transforming spiritual insights?

Tantric sex. This Eastern form of lovemaking is an art, which, if earnestly practiced, is said to transform one's body and soul. The Tantras, or mystical secrets, teach that most of the psychological and physical difficulties in one's life are the result of incorrect sexual attitudes or practices.

When, in centuries past, was the androgynous look popular?

During the Amarna Period in ancient Egypt, especially during the reign of King Akhnaten (circa 1375 B.C.) The King's body and that of his wife, Nefertiti, are depicted very similarly - narrow waists, firm, small breasts and large, rounded buttocks. Men and women in the upper classes imitated the King and Queen and, like them, also appear androgynous wherever they are represented. The reason most commonly given for this practice is that it symbolized the divine unity of both male and female in one body, especially in that of the King.

Being sexually turned on by a shoe is what form of mental disorder?

Fetishism. The mere sight of a given object or a part of the human body, such as a pair of panties or someone's foot or shoe, is enough to sexually arouse the person with that particular fetish.

What recreational clubs, popular in the 1970s, are once again springing up in the U.S.?

Secret clubs for a whole new generation of swingers. The membership is made up of mostly married, younger couples who think that monogamy is an unnatural state and want the option of engaging in sex with others. What goes on in these clubs is legal because it is between consenting adults. The members participate in both "soft swaps" and "hard swaps." The former stops short of full intercourse, the latter doesn't. These clubs are for couples and single women. No solo men allowed and women are said to set the rules for all sexual encounters.

What happened to a married couple if they had sex the night before a Church festival or holy day during the Middle Ages?

They went to hell and were thrown into a lake of boiling pitch, resin and lead for violating the conjugal bed. At least that was the scene conjured up in the *Visions of Alberic* to dissuade Christians from getting too friendly on the eve of red-letter days (Church holy days).

What Roman Emperor liked to have his "lure" nibbled at as he swam around his pool?

Tiberius (42 B.C.-37 A.D.). The nibblers were all young boys. Like a lot of other Roman men, and the Greeks before them, the emperor was a pederast. At the time pederasty was accepted and even promoted as an ideal form of love, especially in Greece.

What are ben-wa balls?

A pair of titillating orbs for milady's pleasure. An inch or so in diameter, ben-wa balls are a Japanese invention originally made of precious metals (gold or silver) and infused with mercury.* When inserted inside a woman's vagina, they are said to provide a source of continual arousal as their mistress walks or moves about. Ben-wa balls are also said to afford any number of terrific hands-off orgasms by rubbing up against a woman's G-Spot. Sound too good to be true? It probably is.

* Many ben-wa balls are now made with chrome or plastic with a counterweight inside, making their pleasure even cheaper.

What counterintuitive activity was once recommended to American women during pregnancy to later prepare them for nursing?

The unlikely recommendation was puppy suckling. In the early 1800s doctors told women that allowing a puppy to nurse at their breast during the third trimester of their pregnancy would strengthen their nipples and improve milk flow. Doctors later moved away from this radical recommendation. A puppy wasn't necessary, they said. The right person would do.

What ex-Marine, who wore red panties and a bra under his uniform, achieved notoriety in the 1940s and 50s directing many hilarious B movies, mostly horror, and dressing in women's clothes?

Edward D. Wood, Jr. All who knew him are quick to clarify that he was not a homosexual or transvestite but a man who just couldn't resist putting on women's clothing now and then. He said it made him feel wonderful. His girlfriend, however, didn't share his enthusiasm. When she found out the lingerie he bought wasn't for her, the relationship hit a snag.

Who spurned all lovers and then fell in love with a watery mirage?

Narcissus.   Haughty and beautiful, he rejected all suitors as unworthy and was condemned by the gods to fall in love with someone his beauty could not seduce. One day while peering into a pool of water he sees a reflection of himself and is instantly smitten. "What shall I do... If I could only escape with my own body."   The bereaved Narcissus dies at the edge of the pool fixated on his own image.   His adoration continues in hell where he will contemplate his likeness in the Stygian waters for eternity.

The men of Niger's Wodaabe nomad tribe use what part of their bodies to charm women and get a bride?

Their eyes – specifically, their right one. Open wide, they roll the eye in and out toward their nose, making themselves look temporarily cock-eyed, a talent Wodaabe women find completely irresistible. Wodaabe men put this ocular ability to full use during what is called the *yaake* dance competition. Beforehand they transform themselves into real beauties with lots of facial make-up, jewelry, colorful embroidered clothing and a turban. Once remade, they preen and parade in front of the tribe's women, then dance for them while rolling their right eye in and out. It's an extremely tense competition with each man hoping to charm at least one of the ladies into marriage.

What Queen of England was said to have yelled downstairs to her household staff, some of whom were reportedly homosexual, "Are there any old queens down there who'll fetch a gin and tonic for an old queen up here"?

The Queen Mum of England, the mother of Queen Elizabeth II. True or not, it's an amusing vignette.

What 1969 best-selling book about sex recommended Coca-Cola for douching?

Everything You Always Wanted To Know About Sex (But Were Afraid To Ask) by Dr. David Reuben. Recently "updated," Dr. Reuben's book now omits the caustic, ill-advised Coca-Cola douche but retains many other benighted passages. As in his 1969 version of the book, he refers to homosexuals as "sexual freaks" and seems to offer a gay man beaten to death with a candlestick as confirmation of his premise.

What operation did Sigmund Freud undergo in order to "rejuvenate" himself?

A vasectomy. Early in the 1900s men sought out the knife in hopes of restoring their male energy. The logic was based on the notion that loss of sperm decreased masculine vitality.

What is an unnatural curvature or bending of the penis called?

Peyronie's disease. The condition is caused by a fibrous infiltration that produces a distortion of the penis when erect. The deformity may or may not be painful and, according to the literature, is not correctable. Because of allegations made in the Paula Jones' deposition against President Bill Clinton, the condition is referred to in some circles as the "president's disease."

Where did women once pay handsomely to restore their "virginity"?

Japan. Thousands of operations were performed on Japanese women in the 1970s and 1980s to restore their hymens. Being that virgin brides were in demand, sheep gut was the membrane of choice used to surgically reconstruct a woman's maidenhead shortly before her wedding. Timing the operation was critical; sheep gut dissolves within a month.

How do the pubescent males of the Caramoja tribe in Uganda permanently lengthen their penises?

By attaching circular stones to their penises frequently weighing upwards of fifteen pounds. The procedure is apparently so successful many of the men then have to tie their wonderments up in knots because the stretched-out penile tissue produces a long, very skinny member.

Note: It is supposedly not uncommon for this stone-lengthening procedure to produce results of up to eighteen inches, or so it is reported.

Why did notable men in ancient Egypt sometimes keep their wives' dead bodies at home for several days before turning them over to the embalmers?

They were afraid the embalmers might sexually violate the deceased, especially if the body were that of a beautiful woman. Herodotus mentions at least one case of an embalmer being caught in flagrante delicto with a corpse. Apparently, waiting a few days helped discourage such violations.

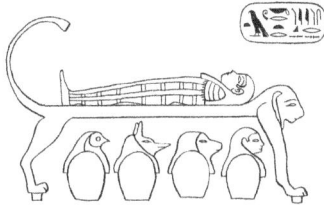

Note: Since the Egyptians believed the dead retained their sexual powers, necrophilia didn't produce the same feelings of outrage then that it does now.

How does the father in some Turkish villages avoid paying the customary "bride-price" when his son is ready to get married?

By arranging a wedding, a double one. Known as a "*berdel*,"* the father of the prospective groom offers a daughter or other female member of his family to his future in-laws. If they accept, the women are exchanged and married the same day to men they most likely have never met. Obviously, in Turkey and other parts of the world where women are routinely swapped as brides the time worn adage, daddy knows best, is still observed.

* "In place of the other" in Kurdish.

What Japanese cartoon genre, increasingly popular in the U.S., means "perversion"?

Hentai. These fantasy pornographic cartoons offer up an array of bizarre characters and X-rated images reportedly capable of shocking even the most jaded. The imported erotica depicts aliens and monsters as well as various demons having their way with childlike women with big eyes and pigtails dressed in high school uniforms.

How did a woman of one East African tribe humiliate her husband if he left her sexually unsatisfied?

By standing outside their hut and yelling that her husband's penis was dead. It's a very amusing story that may not be true. The sourcing on this one is very vague.

Homes in what ancient city had frescoes depicting orgies and lamps shaped like phalli as common decor?

Pompeii. Archeologists and anthropologists originally believed these sites might be brothels. However, after extensive excavation revealing many more structures containing a variety of pornographic motifs, the experts changed their minds. They decided such artwork was simply the decorative choice of most wealthy Pompeiians.

What self-appointed sage of sex observed, "Americans have a bad case of sex in the head, and that's a hell of a place to have it"?

Tallulah Bankhead.

To what do the slang terms Betties, Goolies, Slappers, Love Spuds and the Family Jewels refer?

The testicles.

How does *anhedonia* affect one's life?

Drastically if you have this psychological condition. It refers to the inability to experience pleasure in normally pleasurable ways.

"Whatever our souls are made of, his and mine are the same," is attributed to what poet?

Emily Bronte.

Who said, "Your words are my food, your breath my wine. You are everything to me"?

Sarah Bernhardt.

Who said of sex …"the pleasure is momentary, the position ridiculous, and the expense damnable"?

Lord Chesterton.

Under what conditions might a woman in 16th-century Europe get a divorce?

If her husband were impotent and, as a consequence, she was still a virgin. To prove her virginity she had to submit to an examination by doctors, midwives, and even priests, whose prodding fingers would supposedly verify her hymenal intactness.

What sacred book recommends the stoning of any bride proven not to be a virgin?

The Bible. In Chapter 22, Verses 21 & 22 of *The Book of Deutronomy*, it states that if a bride is accused of not being a virgin then her parents must provide proof she is. Failing such proof, the men of the village stoned the new bride to death in front of her father's house because she had played "the whore in her father's house" and tricked her husband.

What romantic poet kept pubic-hair snippets of his conquests?

Lord Byron aka George Noel Gordon.

118

In centuries past what subterfuge was used to trick interested parties into thinking a woman was a virgin?

A sponge soaked in blood. The ruse was especially popular in brothels where men paid to see women deflowered. Other than the sponge trick, "professional virgins" also used fish bladders filled with blood to produce the desired effect.

What famous 1950s pin-up model stated unabashedly, "God approves of nudity. Adam and Eve in the Garden of Eden, they were naked as jaybirds"?

Secretary turned pin-up girl, Bettie Page.

What is considered to be the average velocity of a male ejaculatory emission?

28 miles per hour according to the March 2008 issue of *Men's Health* magazine. Other sources say less, some say it's more.

Where was the biggest male pornography star of all time discovered?

In a urinal. John Holmes was a supposedly discovered by a man who, after glimpsing his assets, got him into the pornography business. By the late '70s Mr. Holmes was reportedly earning $3,000 a day starring in adult films. The talent that propelled the actor's career is the stuff of legend and not a few raunchy whispers. Though he boasted of a considerably more robust endowment, his wife claimed the object of his bragging was closer to 10 inches.

What famous comedian wittily observed, "Sex at age 90 is like trying to shoot pool with a rope"?

George Burns.

Who wrote the lines, "Love is a smoke raised with the fume of sighs"?

Shakespeare. It is an often quoted line from his play, *Romeo and Juliette*.

What are "golden lilies"?

The severely deformed feet created by the Chinese practice of foot-binding. This cultural tradition is deeply embedded in the Chinese concepts of beauty and sexual attractiveness with the ideal woman's foot easily slipping into a shoe only three to four inches long. Small feet made the woman who had them an object of desire. In fact, it is said that men would more often look at woman's feet initially than at her face. It was believed that such small feet forced the woman to walk in a way that strengthened her vagina, making her even more appealing. It was also believed foot-binding concentrated the nerves sufficiently in the feet so as to turn them into an erogenous zone.

Though no one seems to know for sure, many sources believe the custom began about 1,000 years ago. Whatever its actual beginning, foot-binding was finally outlawed in 1911 – centuries too late for many suffering women. It's easy to understand why the Chinese saying, "Every pair of small feet costs a bath of tears," was no exaggeration. The pain was intense and constant for these women not only from the deformed bones in their feet but from continual infections, even gangrene, that often resulted from their toenails buckling back under their feet and slicing open their skin.

Note: The term, "golden lily," is believed to have originated with a prince who named his concubine's three-inch feet, "*san chun jin lian*," or three-inch golden lily. Lily feet became associated with good breeding and delicacy in China.

What is a pillow book?

Once used by concubines and geishas, the pillow book is filled with graphic sexual pictures designed to stimulate the reader. Not all Japanese pillow books, however, are sexual in nature. Some more resemble diaries or journals that record the owner's thoughts and reflections.

Who gave up his country's crown in 1936 for the love of a commoner?

Edward VIII. Back when royalty was still inclined to frown on tainting its blood with marriage outside its uppity gene pool, Edward VIII abdicated the throne in 1936 saying he simply could not be the King of England without the woman* he loved at his side.

* The American Wallis Simpson was not only a commoner she was also divorced. Neither situation was looked favorably upon by the House of Windsor, the royal house presently headed up by Queen Elizabeth II.

What loud-mouthed American actress observed, "My father warned me about men and booze, but he never mentioned a word about women and cocaine"?

Tallulah Bankhead.

What daring new fashion statement scandalized many international beaches in the 1960s?

The topless swimsuit. Needless to say, designer Rudi Gurnreich's natatorial inspiration made even the most risqué of bikinis look modest by comparison.

What symptoms does a man display when afflicted with "irritable male syndrome"?

Among other things, he gets cranky, nervous, irritable, irrational, depressed, emotional, and even weepy. The syndrome can occur at any age as a result of lowered testosterone levels. Often precipitated by stress, the solution to the syndrome may be more testosterone.

Who fell madly in love with the statue of a woman and implored the heavens to give him a flesh-and-blood wife just like her?

Pygmalion. After sculpting an exquisite ivory statue of a woman, Pygmalion fell in love with his own creation. The statue was so realistic he even began caressing and talking to it, and named it Galatea. In his eyes "she" was the perfect woman. His love for Galatea grew until her stony silence became unbearable to him. Fortunately, the goddess Venus took pity on him and turned Pygmalion's statue into the real thing before he lost his wits altogether.

If you're into *formicophilia*, what are you into?

Deriving pleasure from letting insects crawl around on your skin, frequently the genitals.

If you just love to osculate, what do you love doing?

Kissing. If you want to be romantic, however, asking someone if you can osculate them might not be a good idea. You would probably get thrown back into the nerd pile.

What relatively well-known saxophonist and jazz pianist managed to successfully pass herself off as a man up until his/her death?

Billy Tipton. Billy is said to have fooled everyone, including "his" wives. He supposedly used the "old war injury" excuse to avoid conventional sex with them. Even Tipton's adopted sons supposedly never suspected their father's true sex until his death.

What fragrant evergreen did the Romans regard as a symbol of love?

Myrtle. Venus, the goddess of love, considered it sacred.

What racy internet offering has turned more than one wannabe star into an instant online celebrity?

Uploaded film clips of the bawdy bedroom romps of the not yet famous. After a video showing Paris Hilton having sex hit the web, her 15-minute star was launched into the stratosphere. Instant fans couldn't get enough of her and media rags paid paparazzi top dollar for photos of Ms. Hilton's risqué, not-so-private business.

What movie has the most kisses in it?

The 1926 version of *Don Juan* starring John Barrymore and Mary Astor. They smooched it up, one way or another, a grand total of 127 times.

What famous Victorian wit once commented, "Bigamy is having one wife or husband too many. Monogamy is the same"?

Oscar Wilde.

What famous actress said, "Sex appeal is fifty percent what you've got and fifty percent what people think you've got"?

Sophia Loren.

What reptile mates en masse?

The garter snake, at least one variety does. When the *Thamnophis sirtalis* species emerges from hibernation in the spring, a collective mating occurs. A small number of females and a very large number of males, the latter all vying for sexual favors, aggregate into one big, writhing ball of turned-on snakes.

What species of flower changes sex periodically?

The flower we know as the jack-in-the-pulpit. During some blooming seasons Jack decides to be Jill, especially after lots of rainfall and sunny skies. During drearier years with low rainfall, it is Jack that asserts himself in the pulpit and pollinates.

What man was accused of "botanical pornography"?

Swedish taxonomist, Carolus Linnaeus (1707-1778). Linneaus invented the system for classifying plants and animals. In the case of flowers his contemporaries thought his suggestive nomenclature exceeded all decent limits. For instance, he named one genus of sweet pea "clitoria." Linneaus referred to the stamens of flowers as "husbands," and to the "pistils," as wives. A flower with only one stamen and many pistils was a polygamia. The outrage over Linnaeus's sexually-oriented taxonomy, like pollen, took a while to blow over.

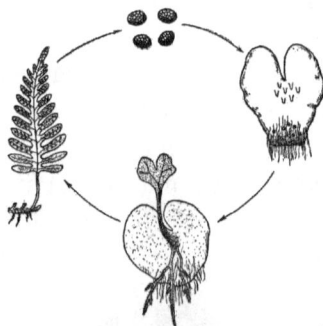

What famous 50s movie star quipped, "I started out to be sex fiend, but I couldn't pass the physical"?

Robert Mitchum.

The Instant Voyeur

Was there ever a time when love was not love?

Love has meant different things in different cultures at different times in history. To the Greeks and Romans love was perceived as a sickness and as a social inconvenience, an impediment to getting ahead in the world. Marriage was entered into to consolidate family interests and to strengthen lineages. Many historians and sociologists point to the so-called Courts of Love that sprang up during the twelfth century as the beginning of romantic love. Apparently, those early songsters or troubadours managed to get everyone so hot and bothered that notions of love took root. It certainly got poor Lancelot and Guinevere in a mess of trouble and proved, in part, to be the undoing of poor King Arthur. Easy to understand - Guinevere was the King's wife. It seems Camelot was not so idyllic after all.

What well known mint is said to heighten the pleasures of oral sex?

Altoids. One reputable online source says maybe yes, maybe no, but basically probably not. In the late 90s the rumor rapidly gained traction and the mint began flying off store shelves everywhere. Whether or not Altoids has any such erogenous attributes, the hype makes for some great come-on lines.

Why did John Lennon and Yoko Ono stage an in-bed media event while on their honeymoon in 1969?

The couple wanted to use the occasion to talk about peace and protest war. At the time the Vietnamese War was escalating.

Note: The couple actually staged two "bed-ins," one in Montreal and the other in Amsterdam. Apparently, the events made a big impression as they are still remembered many years later. However, few seem to recall it was also Lennon and Ono's honeymoon.

What Southwestern fertility symbol is usually depicted as a flute-playing hunchback, seducer of maidens?

The kokopelli. Many colorful tales about this playful figure have evolved over the centuries. He is alternately thought of as a trickster, a rainmaker, a trader and/or a troubadour. In his fertility-symbol role he is sometimes shown with an exaggerated, erect phallus. In one variant of this myth the kokopelli carries seeds or babies in his hump that he offers to young maidens he is hopeful of seducing. Petroglyphs of the flute-playing kokopelli are found on rocks and in caves throughout the Southwest United States.

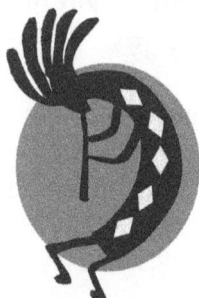

What Hollywood madam gained instant notoriety when her prostitution ring was busted in the mid nineties?

Heidi Fleiss, the famous Madam to the stars, politicos and corporate elite. Convicted and imprisoned for 23 months, Heidi later tried unsuccessfully to start her own brothel in Nevada after being released from jail.

What technological phenomenon has been responsible for many new marriages as well as a fair share of divorces?

Internet amore. Every year more and more people resort to cyberspace to find and woo a potential mate. The smitten vouch for the courting method saying it saves time, money and is a good way to get to know someone before actually meeting them. The number of internet flirtations that end up in marriage is becoming easier to calculate as more people become forthcoming about their cyber encounters. Trolling for sex and love on the internet was once, in the minds of many, the virtual equivalent of a seedy dive where only the desperate would dare venture.

What percentage of women are said to prefer having sex in the dark or with the lights dimmed way down?

The majority.

What contemporary writer asserted, "My lesbianism is an act of Christian charity. There are all those women out there praying for a man, and I'm giving them my share"?

Rita Mae Brown, author of the seminal, lesbian coming- of-age classic, *Rubyfruit Jungle*.

What is an ecdysiast?

It's a fancy word for a striptease artist.

The U.S. is the largest exporter of what unlikely commodity?

Sperm. It's true. In the March 5, 2012 issue of *Time Magazine* an article entitled, "Frozen Assets," confirms that it's in big demand.

What famous actor said of his career, "Every two or three years I knock off for a while. That way I'm constantly the new girl in the whorehouse"?

Robert Mitchum.

What is said to inspire a dead man to have a hard-on?

"Angel lust." At least that it is how it was referred to in a 2001 episode of the HBO series, *Six Feet Under*. Apparently, some guys get real lucky in heaven and end up where all the sexy angels are flitting about.

Which daughter of Queen Isabel and King Ferdinand of Spain carted her dead husband's body around for months before burying him, constantly opening his coffin to make sure he was still there?

Juana La Loca, or Joanna the Crazy, was so was nicknamed because of her obsessive behavior. Deeply in love with and insanely jealous of her husband's flirtations in life, Juana remained so in his death, convinced some woman might still want to steal him away from her.

What famous lovers are confined to the Circle of Lust in Dante's *Divine Comedy*?

Francesca and Paolo*.   In Canto V of the *Divine Comedy*, Francesca confesses how her passion for Paolo led her astray.   She recounts her love affair, blaming the "courtly love" of Lancelot and Guinevere for fueling their ardor and bringing about their downfall.   Now condemned to hell, Francesca finds solace in the thought that she and Paolo will be forever entwined, eternally lovers, saying:

> *Love that exempts no one beloved from loving*
> *caught me so strongly with his charm*
> *that, as you see, it still does not leave me.*
> *Love led us to one death together...*

* Paolo was Francesca's brother-in-law.   Francesca's husband, Giovanni, found and killed them both somewhere around 1285.   Speculation has it that Dante may have wanted to rehabilitate Francesca's memory out of respect for her family, a prominent one in Ravenna, Italy.

What famous scientist made the following observation, "Women marry men hoping they will change. Men marry women hoping they will not. So each is inevitably disappointed"?

Albert Einstein.

What face launched a 1,000 ships, a passionate love affair and a very long war?

Helen of Troy, considered the most beautiful woman in the world in Greek mythology. Her beauty so beguiled a youth named Paris (the son of Priam, King of Troy) that he abducted her from her much older and powerful husband, Menelaus, the King of Sparta, and whisked her away to live with his family in Troy. Though Helen supposedly went willing, more than a few problems followed the star-crossed pair – like the legendary warrior, Achilles *, and half the Greek army. After many failed attempts at capturing Troy and recovering Helen, the gift of a huge Trojan Horse was used as a ruse to get inside the city walls. Greek warriors secretly concealed in the horse emerged from it at night to capture Troy and restore Helen to her husband with whom, according to one account, she lived happily ever after. Who knows? Maybe all the strum and drang in Troy finally just got to her.

* Brad Pitt played him in the 2004 movie, *Troy*.

Note: Paris and Helen's love affair is the stuff of myth and legend. There is some controversy, however, as to the Battle of Troy and whether it actually happened. A few historians believe it might have since myths often have some basis in fact. If that's the case, then perhaps Paris and Helen do as well.

Is there such a thing as a sex-after-death or a "farewell intercourse law"?

The Egyptian parliament was reportedly considering the passage of such a bill as of April, 2012. If enacted it would grant men the legal right to have sex with their wives up to six hours after they died. Why the cutoff was set at the sixth hour is not known. Women, apparently, would also enjoy the same legal right as their husbands - how it would be accomplished in their case is not entirely clear. Egypt's National Council for Women appealed to parliament not to make the bill into law. What ultimately happened with this legislation is now a bit of a mystery or, perhaps, just another example of another embargoed story. Alternatively, maybe the story was fiction from the get go.

Who was listed as the oldest living married couple in the 2011 Guinness Book of Records?

Herbert and Zelmyra Fisher of James City, N.C. As of February 14, 2011, the couple had been married 86 years. Zelmyra, 103, and her husband, Herbert, 105, said at the time there was no particular secret as to the longevity of their marriage. One of their grandchildren thinks it is because the Fishers took their vows seriously, sticking it out through thick and thin, good times and bad.

Note: Herbert Fisher died February, 2011, three months short of the Fishers' 87th anniversary on May 13th.

What is *philematology*?

The science or study of kissing. Yes, it has become a subject deemed worthy of serious consideration. Among other things researchers look at how *oxytocin*, a hormone associated with feelings of love, is affected by kissing. Scientists are also interested in just what way kissing may subconsciously transmit certain information about their partner's biology and immune system. While there are experts that argue kissing may help promote the survival of our species, others say no, pointing out that ten percent, possibly more, of the world doesn't engage in the activity at all.

Where did kissing once carry the death penalty?

According to some sources, it did in 16th-century Italy – in Naples to be exact. Locking lips there led to the gallows.

What woman pointed out that "The difference between pornography and erotica is lighting"?

Gloria Leonard, a one time busy actress in the porn industry who went on to become the publisher of *High Society* magazine known for featuring hardcore layouts of nude models. Faithful to Leonard's take on the visual, these shoots were no doubt done without erotic lighting.

The world's longest engagement lasted for how many years?

Most online sources put it at 67. That's how many years Octavio Guillen and Adriana Martinez put off their marriage before they tied the knot. The Mexican couple got engaged in 1902 and finally wed in 1969. Why the two kept delaying their wedding day is not entirely clear. Perhaps they liked the idea of a long engagement and/or thought that getting married might take the romance out of their relationship. Who knows? Maybe they just ran out of excuses.

What Supreme Court Justice defended a person's First Amendment right to read or to view pornography if they so desired?

William O. Douglas. He railed against government censorship and the confusion the Supreme Court created with its obscenity rulings. In a 1960s case, *The Right of The People*, he wrote..."The idea of using obscenity to bar thoughts of sex is dangerous. A person without sex thoughts is abnormal....." Douglas thought it abhorrent that people might be charged and convicted of obscenity when the word itself couldn't be defined with any precision. In the 1973 *Miller v. California** he wrote that "To send men to jail for violating standards they cannot understand, construe, and apply is a monstrous thing to do in a Nation dedicated to fair trials and due process.

* In this case the Supreme Court created guidelines for jurors in obscenity trials called the "Miller Test." Simply put, it helped prosecutors pursue convictions for obscenity applying vague legal standards.

What surprising item do vending machines in Japan offer for sale?

The cast-off underwear of schoolgirls. At least they did in the 1990s when a pair of used panties sold for around fifty U.S. dollars. As shocking as it may seem to those outside of Japan, the panties were often accompanied by pictures of their former owners.

Has there ever been a brothel that specifically catered to senior citizens?

Yes. One of the first to conduct business was raided by police in 1975. According to the newspaper, *The Montreal Gazette,* the raid in Marseilles, France turned up eight men ranging in age from 60 to 77 and two prostitutes in their 50s. Apparently the brothels helped out its clientele in more ways than one. The newspaper said that since old-age pensions in France averaged only about $4 a day, the $10 service charge was a bargain. So called over-the-hill brothels are now pretty much *au courant* just about everywhere in the world. It seems Viagra has been a real boon to the whorehouse business whether they are geared to old geezers or not. It makes one wonder what those guys back in Marseilles did without the help of a little blue pill. Could it be they just didn't need it back then?

What advice does *The Bible* offer on love?

"Love is patient, love is kind. It does not envy, it does not boast, it is not proud. It is not rude, it is not self-seeking, it is not easily angered, it keeps no record of wrongs. ... It always protects, always trusts, always hopes, always perseveres." - *Corinthians*

Is a "pharmaceutical love drug" possible?

According to some researchers, it is within the realm of possibility. In the future drugs may be available that will make people want to be closer to each other. Whether they mean physically or emotionally, or both, is not clear. Until it is, along with a working definition of love, playing around with the brain's love circuitry could be a bit problematical. Unintended consequences are written all over this one.

How old is the oldest known sculpture of a female nude?

Sources claim 22,000 to 25,000 years young according to the latest estimates. Called the "Venus of Willendorf,"* the corpulent female nude is actually a figurine about four-and-one-half inches high. The woman is reminiscent of how Fernando Botero sculpts and paints the female body – lardy and obese but not entirely without charm, depending on your point of view.

* Discovered in Austria in 1908, the Venus of Willendorf's female attributes are all clearly visible. As a result, when a Tempe, Arizona artist, Bill Tonnesen, recently sculpted a larger than life statue of the iconic figurine in 2012, he got a lot of flack from a church across the street as well as from his wife. In a conciliatory move, he adorned the Venus's private parts with dollar bills. The logic of which is not entirely clear since some people felt it now made his version of the Venus of Willendorf look like a fat stripper.

When was the first onscreen kiss between two women?

It's hard to source for sure but it was most likely in Cecil Demille's 1922 movie, *Manslaughter*. A gratuitous orgy scene also appeared in the film. Most movie buffs consider this picture Demille's least noteworthy cinematic effort.

When was the first onscreen kiss between two men?

In the 1927 Oscar winner for best picture, *Wings*. The silent movie shows two soldiers kissing each other on the mouth while waiting in the trenches to do battle in World War I. There was reportedly no public hue and cry over the scene as it was assumed such things went on during the war.

What museum offers an after-hours "naturist tour" with naked guides and guards leading the way through the artwork?

The MONA, Museum of Old and New Art, outside of Hobart, Tasmania, beside the Derwent River. Just opened in January of 2011 the private museum is home to a multimillion dollar collection of what has been described as edgy and subversive art with an emphasis on sex and death. The "naturist tour" must be reserved ahead of time and promises a unique experience for all who dare doff their clothes and follow the guides through dimly lit corridors lined with controversial artwork. At the end of the tour the attendees end up in a brightly lit room lined with mirrors where their nakedness becomes part of a living art exhibit. Esthetics is not at the forefront of this graphic exercise in conceptual art. It is said that uptight attitudes about nudity and perfection quickly melt away under the glaring light of reality.

Polari is the slang, or "secret tongue," once used by what socially ostracized group?

Gay men in the London and other British cities during the first two-thirds of the twentieth century. Being that homosexuality was rigorously prosecuted at the time men developed a secret way of communicating with each other. _Polari*_ was a rich, vibrant "language" borrowed from different sources over many decades, some say centuries.

Why was Alan Turing, the man who cracked the "Enigma Code" in World War II, injected with female hormones in 1952?

Prosecuted for "gross indecency" (legal code for being homosexual), Turing opted for hormone shots rather than going to prison. He committed suicide in 1954.

Note: The injections were thought to be a possible cure for homosexuality. Britain didn't want its premier cryptanalyst consorting with "perverts."

What major scandal rocked the Secret Service in 2012?

Members of the Secret Service advance team awaiting President Obama's trip to Cartagena, Colombia, in April of 2012 decided to have a little fun and invited some local prostitutes back to their hotel. At least one of agents apparently had quite a dust-up with the lady who serviced him when he didn't want to pay her what she thought she deserved. Being that prostitution is legal in Colombia the complaining woman took her grievances directly to the police who then notified American authorities. "Dania," as the woman calls herself, stated that had she been a spy wanting to get "sensitive information" from the agent it would not have been difficult. She also claimed that during their *tête-à-tête*, or whatever you want to call it, she had access to the agent's wallet while he was passed out from an alcohol-induced stupor. The scandal's embarrassment to the administration resulted in not a few firings, early retirements, and apologies by those involved. A new set of ethics classes are now scheduled for all members of the Secret Service. Additionally, supervisors will accompany most future advance teams to make sure the boys behave according to a new code of conduct.

Note: Several members of the military and the DEA were also involved in the scandal.

What is considered one of the most famous onscreen kisses ever?

The one in the film classic, *Casablanca,* when Ingrid Bergman turns to Humphrey Bogart and says, "Kiss me, kiss me as if it were the last time."

What famous iconic actress said, "A kiss is a lovely trick designed by nature to stop speech when words become superfluous"?

Ingrid Bergman.

What sensuous Rodin sculpture was said to have been inspired by the eternally entwined lovers, Francesca and Paolo, in Dante's *Divine Comedy*?

The Kiss.

The Instant Voyeur

Other Invisibird Books in the Instant Series by Tanya Slover:

> *The Instant Genius: An Indispensable Handbook for Know-It-Alls*
> *The Instant Celebrity: Their 15 Minutes of Fame, Notoriety or Whatever*
> *The Instant Politico: Memorable Scandals, Secrets and Gaffes**
> *The Instant Idiot: Dumbest Things People, Famous or Not, Have Said or Done**

* Forthcoming

Invisibird Books for Children:

The Adventures of Billy the Cat

Tanya Slover is an author, poet and screenwriter. She has also ghostwritten for doctors and has a background in anthropology.

Invisibird
Books